Beating men at their own game

Beating men at their own game

A Woman's Guide to Successful Selling in Industry

RICHARD H. BUSKIRK
The Herman W. Lay Chair of Marketing
Southern Methodist University

BEVERLY MILES
Publisher and Owner
Intowner Magazine
Parkhurst Publications
Dallas, Texas

JOHN WILEY & SONS
New York • Chichester • Brisbane • Toronto

This publication is designed to provide accurate and
authoritative information in regard to the subject
matter covered. It is sold with the understanding that
the publisher is not engaged in rendering legal, accounting,
or other professional service. If legal advice or other
expert assistance is required, the services of a competent
professional person should be sought. *From a Declaration
of Principles jointly adopted by a Committee of the
American Bar Association and a Committee of Publishers.*

Library of Congress Cataloging in Publication Data

Buskirk, Richard Hobart, 1927-
    Beating men at their own game.

    1. Industrial procurement.   2. Women sales
personnel.   I. Miles, Beverly, joint author.   II. Title.
HF5437.B87   658.8'5'024042   80-12337
ISBN 0-471-05325-2

Printed in the United States of America

10 9 8 7 6 5 4 3 2 1

To our subjects—the thousands of women who sell goods and services to industrial purchasing agents, merchants, wholesalers, professional people of all sorts, and the multitude of government agencies. For want of a better term we call them the industrial saleswomen.

Foreword

This very exciting book gives an extra dimension to the working arena for women. Women have been excellent salespersons for generations. Witness, for example, the predominantly female work force of women in retail selling.

This book is not about the retail salesperson but about industrial selling, for example, selling cosmetics, food products, furniture, computers, carpeting, and so on. Even though the techniques may not vary too much between the woman who sells a $10,000 mink and a lathe, the woman who goes into the field should learn about lathes if she is going to sell them. Can she do it? The authors answer convincingly with a strong affirmative. She not only can, but there are enough women pioneers who have proved that they can do so. Are there obstacles to overcome? Just as any job worth its salt, this job is no easy one. But it is not easy for a man either. Traveling, rearing a family, and keeping a household together have always been part of the role of successful women executives and managers. In fact, the industrial salesperson has more leeway to manage her time than an ordinary management job. The woman salesperson's earnings in this field far outweigh any disadvantages she may have in taking a more routine job.

Some women may still be troubled about how men will react to their invading and competing in a man's territory. Again, as in other areas of management, well-adjusted, successful men do not worry about the competition. In fact, many of them welcome women who are willing to compete on equal terms. Do not, say the authors, expect special favors because you are a woman, but be reassured that if you are successfull men will not resent you. In fact, some of them will ask how you accomplish what you do. It may take courage to go into this relatively new area, but the end result is well worth the effort.

The authors speak with authority because they have been there. They are willing to share their joint experiences in a very readable and informative fashion.

The book should be a welcome addition to marketing courses at universities, to counseling services, and to women's groups that are always anxious to pursue new avenues for women. The illustrations are clear, practical, and interesting. They lend an air of authenticity to the study that might otherwise be lacking. I like the appendix, which furnishes several selling incidents that can be readily adopted to case studies for discussion in classes, seminars, or college courses.

In all this book is worth reading—and besides you will enjoy it.

Edith M. Lynch

Partner, Lynch Associates
February 1980

Preface

This book resulted from the mating of my academic curiosity with my practical need to know much more about what happens to women who enter industrial selling. I had observed two distinct trends. First, my classes in selling and sales management had become popular among the women whereas only a few years ago few women would have taken such courses. Second, I noticed that large industrial concerns were hiring women for their sales forces. From an academic standpoint I had to know more about how they were doing, the problems they were encountering, the problems managements were having integrating women into their sales forces, and how the field of selling and sales management would change with the advent of the bisexual sales forces. Moreover, as an author, I had the practical need to know about women in selling in order to incorporate the information into my books *Management of the Sales Force, 5th edition* (Homewood, Ill.: Richard D. Irwin, Inc., 1979) and *Textbook of Salesmanship*, 10th edition (New York: McGraw-Hill, 1979).

It has been a very worthwhile experience. As the perceptive reader may well guess, most of the problems that one might expect the women to encounter in the sales world proved less troublesome than I had at first anticipated.

To write this book together, co-author Beverly Miles and I had to make several editorial decisions regarding format. We felt it best that we clearly identify to the reader who was writing what words. Thus two different typefaces are used to distinguish which of us is speaking. Additionally, the saleswomen are quoted in still another typeface. Thus three typefaces appear throughout this book.

We have written a book about women in industrial selling, not a book about how to sell. There are many excellent books on the technical aspects of salesmanship that apply equally to men and women. We are more interested in preparing the woman for the personal, psychological side of the sales job.

Finally, I wish to thank my two research assistants, June Shafer and Marsha Kolar, for their significant contributions to this work.

Dallas, Texas   RICHARD H. BUSKIRK
February 1980

I am delighted to have been asked to co-author this book. I believe one can do only one thing with experience and knowledge—share it. Relating the many experiences I have had over the years in a field that was once almost totally dominated by men has given me many fond memories and much amusement. I hope this book will inspire those women who think they might benefit from a career in sales. I hope it will also act as an incentive for ambitious women to use their intellectual ability, their creativity, and their drive to the fullest—for as Betty Frieden, author of The Feminine Mystique, *wrote in 1963: "The only way for a woman, as for a man, to find herself, to know herself as a person, is by creative work of her own."*

According to an article that appeared on January 15, 1979, in U.S. News & World Report, titled "The Joys and Sorrows of Working Women," women are swelling the work force at a rate of almost 2 million every year. Every field and occupation is being entered by women, who are pouring into the job market almost twice as fast as men.

The article stated that President Carter has chosen women for 38 percent of his appointments to federal jobs paying $26,222 or more annually and has cracked down on job discrimination. He has encouraged the government to develop new programs to prepare women for high-paying jobs normally held by men.

A popular advertising campaign banners the headline, "You've come a long way, baby," reflecting the mood of women nationwide as they enter areas unthought of a few years earlier. Women are now routinely serving in the cabinet, attending military academies, sailing with the navy, managing corporations, or climbing telephone poles for AT&T.

Women still, on the average, earn less than men. Male high school dropouts earn on the average $1704 more per year than the average woman college graduate. The article in U.S. News & World Report *stated that nearly 80 percent of all the women working are employed in the traditional clerical, service, or light factory jobs.*

According to a business research organization—The Conference Board—even though the federal government is the largest employer of women, these very women hold 76 percent of the lowest-paying federal jobs. Only 3.2 percent of federal jobs pay more than $42,000 per year. A nurse may earn only half as much as a bus driver, flight attendants are paid less than the men who clean the airplanes, and office workers do not earn as much as janitors.

The Conference Board reports that three-fourths of all working women are employed in services, finance, insurance, real estate, retail trades, and light factory work while men dominate construction, mining, transportation, and heavy manufacturing. Although women hold a majority of industrial jobs they are seldom in positions of management. The Conference Board found that women hold more than 80 percent of the clerical jobs in banking; yet they hold less than 20 percent of the management positions.

The sales field has recently opened its doors to women. And it is an area where a woman's success depends on her ability, determination, and courage.

Women entering today's sales force come mainly from four categories: the college graduate, bored housewife, dissatisfied secretary, and the woman acting out of desperation.

The sales arena, previously a male-dominated field,

*offers the woman many challenges. Some of these
challenges will stem from her male co-workers'
misconceptions concerning the effect that her femininity
will have in relation to her job and customers. Some other
challenges will stem from the woman's own lack of
knowledge concerning her own abilities and a lack of
knowledge about the workings within the business world.
She may have to overcome an initial bias not related to her
sexuality. Like people everywhere she may have a negative
image regarding salespeople. The word "salesman" may
bring to mind the shady, fast-talking, unreliable con artist
so commonly associated with the word "sales." At least, the
image often brings to mind the stereotyped picture of the
drummer or peddler who slapped backs and passed out
catalogs and cigars on a yearly visit to customers.*

*The purpose of this book is to help the woman entering
this exciting field to look objectively at herself, to become
aware of the skills she needs for success, and to acquire a
better understanding of her role in the business world.*

*I give a debt of gratitude to my dear friend LuLu
Hammond whose support and encouragement made my
portion of this book possible.*

Dallas, Texas   BEVERLY MILES
February 1980

Contents

Industrial Saleswomen   1

  Different Buyer-Seller Relationships   4
  Lower Selling Costs   5
  Freedom   6
  Management Potentiality   7
  Success Leads to More Success   8
  The Mythology of Selling   9

What is a Salesperson?   16

  Some Basic Philosophies   17
  Self-Confidence   18

What Kind of Sales Job is for You?   26

  Home and Family Restraints   26
  Pay Demands   28
  Travel Constraints   29
  Educational Restraints   33
  Your Threshold of Boredom   33
  Personal Goals   34
  Nature of the Job   35
  Personal Freedom   36
  Relationship with Superiors   37
  Need for Training   38
  Mobility   38

What to Look for in an Industrial Sales Job . . .   40

  Training Program   40
  Office Support   42

Compensation Plans   43
Transfer Policy   44
Fellow Salespeople   45
History   46
Firm's Reputation with Customers   46
Financial Stability   46
Attitude of Superior   47
Fringe Benefits   48
Are there Other Women Already in the Sales Force?   49

What is Expected of You by Your Boss?   **51**

Follow Orders   51
Company Loyalty   52
Company Policy   53
Territorial Responsibility   54
Work Discipline   54
Be on Call   55

Getting Promoted   **57**

Go Where There Are Opportunities to Be Promoted   57
Performance   58
Proving Managerial Talents   59
Paperwork   60
Suggestions   60
Recruiting Personnel   61
Training   62
Company Practices   62
Changing Jobs   62

Management of Personal Affairs   **63**

Self-Development   67
Reading   67
Educational Programs   68

Peer Group Learning   68
Post-Sale Evaluations   69

Basic Personality Traits Leading to Success   **71**

Mental Toughness   72
Mental Toughness versus Fear   75
Social Intelligence   80
Acceptance of Responsibility   81
Commitment   84
Motivation   85

What is Success?   **89**

How to Win   **96**

Look Like a Winner   96
Associate with Winners   97
If You Can't Win, Don't Play   97
Success Is Learned   98
Cop-outs   100
The Taste of Winning   101
Hustle   102
Winning: A Matter of Percentages or Skill?   103

Fear of Loss of Femininity   **106**

To Choose or not to Choose   **114**

Women versus Little Girls   **118**

Industrial Saleswomen: Where Do They Come From?   **122**

Bored Housewife   122
Secretary   129
Desperate Woman   134
College Graduate   140

Games Women Often Play That Do Little for Success in Selling   **145**

   Poor Little Me   146

   Seduction   148

   Cute Little Girl   151

   Take Care of Me   152

   Play Child   153

   Chip on the Shoulder   154

   Spoiled Child   157

Conclusion   **159**

Appendix A   **161**

   Some Selling Incidents   161

   Answers to Incidents   168

Appendix B   **179**

   Information on the Survey of Industrial Saleswomen   179

Appendix C   **184**

   Test Yourself: Are You Cut Out for a Sales Career?   184

Appendix D   **188**

   A Short Course in Selling   188

Beating men at their own game

Industrial saleswomen

Welcome to the world of selling. Until now it's been largely a man's world for several reasons irrelevant to our discussion. *Industrial sales representatives* sell goods and services to business firms that in some way use them to create other goods and services that are ultimately sold to the consumer. It includes selling to such firms as manufacturers, wholesalers, retailers, professional people, institutions, governmental agencies, and a multitude of institutions that support business such as accounting firms, advertising agencies, and credit bureaus. The *retail salesperson* sells to the ultimate consumer who buys to use the goods or service. The fact is that industrial selling is no longer exclusively a man's world. Women now successfully sell all sorts of industrial goods. The numbers of women in this field multiply rapidly as success brings about success. There are good reasons for believing that women will play an even larger and more significant role in the nation's industrial sales force.

First, there has never been a plentiful supply of good salespeople. Skilled salespeople are scarce, always have been. Although there are all sorts of people carrying sample cases who travel around in cars and try to pass themselves off as salesreps many are imposters who hold their jobs simply because they're the best of the poor lot from which they were chosen. Indeed, the labor pool from which people are selected for sales jobs has been too small, far too small, for the liking of sales managers who strongly prefer to look at many high-quality people before filling a vacancy. The reasons for this small labor pool are not difficult to pinpoint, but money is certainly not one of them. Sales positions pay relatively well. The culprit is elsewhere. It lies in the nature of the work and its general social status.

Many sales jobs require considerable traveling. The salesrep must be away from home for long periods of time while contacting the trade. This is not true of a large number of industrial salespeople; still it is true of a sufficient number that the general public has the idea that salespeople are away from home a lot. Thus the people who don't want to lead this type of life shun a sales career.

Moreover, the salesperson does not rate high in our status hierarchy. While most people brag about being doctors, lawyers, bankers, or even thieves, only the very professional, the most skilled salesreps brag about their job. Indeed, many companies try to disguise their sales force by calling them company representatives, district managers, field editors, and all sorts of other euphemisms to disguise the fact that the people are peddlers.*

Status is important to most people. Time and again they will work at reduced wages for prestigious titles with prestigious companies. People want to feel important and they want other people to think they are important. Most people fail to understand the importance of the sales job in our economy—its economic role and functions. Industrial salesreps are a vital cog in our socioeconomic system because they provide much-

---

*The word "peddler" was used particularly to illustrate that such synonyms for salespeople (others are huckster, pushers, or drummer) are generally considered derogatory by most people.

needed information and service to customers who have problems that can be solved with the salesrep's products. Unless those problems are solved, the enterprise will suffer severe losses.

And then there is the matter of the job security that most people seek. They want to be sure of their jobs. They don't like the pressure of having to produce results daily. One of the hallmarks of selling is that its performance is easily measurable—How much did you sell? How much money did you bring into the company coffers today?

There's no place for the inept individual to hide in selling. Selling is for people who can produce. People who are not confident of their abilities flee from sales jobs. They fear that their weaknesses will be quickly discovered. This is most unfortunate because, as we will soon see, many of these people would make excellent sales representatives with the proper training.

With the advent of women into the labor pool for industrial sales jobs, sales managers in the future will be looking at not only a larger number of people, but also higher quality ones. In the long run, the increasing numbers of women in industrial sales forces will logically upgrade the quality of those forces. The marginal man who would have been hired in previous years will be edged out by a woman whose abilities promise to be superior. Thus it is to management's distinct advantage that large numbers of women seek industrial sales positions.

And as we shall soon see, women are rapidly discovering what selling has to offer them. Moreover, the new career woman is less intimidated by the selling environment than her mother was. Let's now examine what women have going for them in selling.

Different Buyer-Seller Relationships

Because of the latent sexual overtones of all man-woman social relationships, the male will continually treat a woman differently—and usually with more consideration—than he will other males. In our Dallas study of industrial saleswomen (discussed in Appendix B) the respondents said they felt they were able to get in to see prospective buyers easier—and were treated with more deference than would be the case with a salesman. Where a purchasing agent might be rude to a man, our cultural upbringing, combined with natural biological inclinations, usually encourage him to give the saleswoman maximum opportunity.

Saleswoman—Business Systems

I think women in sales have a distinct advantage in getting to make their sales presentations. I get in a lot more doors than the guys do. I found that when you walk in a door and ask for Mr. So and So the secretary may try to block you, but when this guy sees a young woman asking for him, curiosity usually gets the better of him; so he'll invite you in his office.

Indeed, biological and psychological theories predict that the male purchasing agent may subconsciously, and even consciously, want to buy from the saleswoman as a possible means of seducing her, even though the seduction never takes place. "I'll give you what you want; now give me what I want" is the implicit proposition. As many women have often observed, "Men are always on the make." This is a case of simply using that basic predisposition toward the female to a legal commercial advantage. Interestingly, it is not really the female who is being seduced, but rather the male purchasing agent.

Our Dallas saleswomen have found that if an overt proposition is handled in an offhand, I-know-you-were-joking manner and the discussion is turned back to business, the prospective buyer immediately gets down to the work at hand and listens to what the woman has to say. It's the knowledge and expertise that make the sales—not the sex.

It may be interesting to observe during the next few years if corporate management will use women as purchasing agents as a defensive countertactic to the industrial saleswoman. We know little about how women in business react to other women. No doubt a study of the topic is in the future.

Lower Selling Costs

While wages are rapidly rising for top-flight industrial salespeople, some managements trying to hold down selling costs, may automatically hire more and more women. Often the wage rejected by a male as too low is considered by many women to be most handsome. Thus some male industrial salesmen may price themselves out of some markets.

Our Dallas study clearly showed that our industrial saleswomen got into selling because the job paid more money than they could earn elsewhere. The women could make higher earnings in selling than elsewhere. Consequently, what looks like poor money to many men, looks like good money to most women whose wages in the "traditional" women's jobs have been relatively low.

One of the aspects the women most liked about selling was that they were paid commensurate with what they produced, the same as the men. If the job paid a 5 percent commission, then everyone got 5 percent.

Saleswoman—Business Systems
I love sales. I love the independence. I like the money I make. I've doubled my salary in nine months. I essentially work my own hours. There are fewer conflicts with the people you work with because you hardly ever see them. I enjoy meeting people and I love just everything about selling. I feel it's a great field for women to be in. I wouldn't want a sales job where I was gone Monday through Friday because I've got so many things going on, activities in the community, that I wouldn't want to spend my life in a hotel room.

Freedom

The saleswomen reported that they had discovered one virtue offered by selling—the freedom to manage one's own time. Homemakers, particularly, commented about how they were able to weave their homemaking responsibilities around their sales jobs. When needed at home, they could usually get free to be there and still be able to cover their sales territory as demanded.

Saleswoman—Microfilm Equipment
I have a fortunate situation where I have a lady who comes to the house to baby-sit my children. Previously, I had them in a school; so when they got sick, I had to miss work. You need to have good baby-sitting. People understand that you need time off when your children are sick, but there's a limit. If you're living in a city where your mother or mother-in-law lives it's better—just so you have somebody to depend on when you need help. It's costing me about $300 a month for baby-sitting. You have to be willing to make that sacrifice because as far as I'm concerned the kids come first.

Saleswoman—Business Systems
I hate anything to do with the house and my mother was the same way. I don't like to cook or clean. I'm just an outside person. When we were dating my husband was well aware of that; he doesn't mind doing that stuff; so we split it and it works out great. If I cook, he does the dishes or vice versa. He's an immaculate housekeeper and I'm not; so I've learned

to upgrade my standards a little bit and he's very relaxed about the way things look. It works out pretty well.

Sales Manager—Wholesale and Retail Grocery Supplier
With a woman, if she has a husband who expects supper on the table at a certain time, she's got a problem, because we expect our work to be done first. This is something I point out to women very strongly when I interview them for a job. I can tell you that from the standpoint of the company we don't have lower standards for women. We pay them the same salary as men, but we also expect the same work done.

Management Potentiality

When formulating the study of saleswomen in Dallas, we hypothesized that a large number of the women entered selling because they had realized it was a likely route into general management. The history of career women in management has largely been one of working in highly specialized staff positions that generally lead nowhere. True, these staff jobs can be prestigious and fairly well paid; still women who want general management jobs were frustrated in their aspirations. In most corporations, the way to the top is either through production or sales. For women it would seem that sales would be the most likely route, or so we reasoned— which shows how much we knew about it.

This hypothesis was not sustained. Few women had managerial aspirations. They liked the jobs they were doing. They were professional saleswomen—and seemed likely to remain so because of their own inclinations.

The woman who had managerial hopes seemed likely to have them fulfilled. A top industrial saleswoman for Eastman Kodak, she voiced a strong desire to be promoted into management. This woman's superiors said she was to be promoted in two months.

Success Leads to More Success

Finally, as the successful record of the first generation of industrial saleswomen becomes known to other women, it seems likely that an ever-increasing number will be attracted to selling. This theory is supported indirectly by the biggest reason women fail in selling.

The Dallas survey clearly indicated that the biggest problem women face in selling is their own insecurity and lack of confidence in their ability to sell. With experience, these insecurities and lack of self-confidence will disappear.

Saleswoman—Copying Equipment

As far as looking back ten years ago I would say my lack of confidence was probably my major limiting factor. I probably acted much more confidently than I really was because everybody tends to look at you and say, "Oh, this will never last," and it kind of put me on the defense.

As more and more women succeed in industrial selling—and as their success becomes visible—other women will be encouraged to enter the field. Moreover, much of this insecurity and lack of self-confidence is rooted in the past. After all, women are new to this male-dominated world of business. They don't know much about it yet and are highly intimidated at every turn. As they gain experience, this intimidation will diminish. They will learn that they can compete successfully in the business world. When this happens, selling will seem far less fearsome to the average career woman than it does at present. Old relationships and roles are changing. The young woman coming from school today is not a captive of tradition. She has far more confidence in her ability to succeed in the business world than did her mother and grandmother—all of which means that industrial selling is in for an interesting future.

The Mythology of Selling

Many people shun selling careers because they believe the mythology that surrounds sales jobs. Let us examine and debunk these myths. When we finish we hope that you have a better idea of what selling is like.

Myth One—*Salespeople Are Born, Not Made*

Practically every large company that has developed a hard-hitting sales force has done so by training willing individuals to be good salespeople. Most such companies want no part of the so-called born salesman, for he is apt to be an aggressive bore trying to get by on what he feels is a "winning" personality.

We know salespeople can be made (trained), for this is done all the time. All that is required is someone who wants to become a salesperson and has a reasonably workable personality.

If you deeply feel you are either born with selling skills or not, then you will not apply yourself to learning the skills the salesperson must acquire. Make up your mind that you can learn to sell if you want to do so.

Myth Two—*Good Salespeople Are Good Talkers*

Good salespeople are good listeners. Selling is the art of asking the right questions—questions which lead the prospect's thinking process toward the conclusion that the salesperson's proposition will solve the problem at hand.

When the customer talks you:

1. Learn what the customer wants.

2. Learn what the customer is like.
3. Have time to think about the sale.
4. Make the customer feel important, thus building up his or her ego.

When you, the salesperson, talk:

1. You feel great.
2. The customer is apt to be bored.
3. You're not likely to get the sale.

So learn how to get the customer to talk about what you want to hear.

Myth Three—*The Good Salesperson Can Sell Anything*

There are all sorts of top-notch industrial salespeople who would do badly in retail selling. Just because an individual is great at selling used cars does not mean this same person would sell apparel with equal success. A great computer salesperson would not necessarily be successful selling advertising.

Great salespeople seem to love the goods they sell. They have a certain attachment or fondness for their wares that they convey to the prospect. Mike Schwartz, owner-manager of Nina Carron, a fabric store in Dallas, relates how everyone in his family laughed at his father's and grandfather's devotion to their goods. They actually hated to sell some fine fabrics because it was like parting with an old friend. Mike's love for those fabrics is communicated to the prospect as he talks about the goods. In fact, Mike has some of the world's finest cashmere fabrics in stock (at $235 a yard) almost solely for his own enjoyment.

The point is that you must find the type of goods about which you can develop some enthusiasm. If you don't like what you are selling, then stop selling it and find something you do like. If you can't find anything you enjoy selling, then perhaps another profession would be advisable.

Myth Four—*A Good Salesperson Can Sell to Anyone*
A good salesperson spends his or her time with good prospects—people who need the product and have the money to buy it. Why bother with all the effort of trying to sell your product to someone who neither needs nor can afford it.

The salesperson who insists on trying to twist the arm of some poor person who does not want or need the item is not a salesperson. This is a confidence man or extortionist.

Myth Five—*The Fun and Games Myth*
Folklore as propagated by the plethora of traveling salesman jokes has the salesman continually on the road flitting from one tryst to another. While some salespeople must travel, most don't. Since industrial selling is largely concentrated in large urban centers, the amount of traveling by the average industrial sales representative is modest. Most of them are home regularly and lead normal family lives.

Myth Six—*Selling Is a Life of Wining and Dining*
Some entertainment is required in some selling jobs, but several factors in the current scene limit the amount of entertaining. First, because of the absurdly high costs of entertaining, companies are doing less of it today than previously. Second, in this era in which bribery and buyer-seller relationships are carefully scrutinized, sellers are being far more discreet in their entertainment of customers. Third, IRS regulations have had a signif-

icant impact on entertainment practices. The income tax people dislike the fact that taxpayers have been overly extravagant in entertaining some customers. Tax agents are carefully auditing expense accounts and examining entertainment expenditures to determine the purpose of the entertainment, where it took place, who was being entertained, and the amount spent.

Initially, management was apprehensive about how women would be able to entertain male customers. All sorts of obvious problems came to mind. The potentialities for big trouble with good customers was truly frightening to many sales managers. And many women wondered how they would handle the entertainment aspects of selling. Even more seriously, they wondered if they would be able to handle the customer who wanted to be overly friendly as a condition for giving an order.

We now have some experience with these problems, and as is usually the case with such fears, they prove to be more fantasy than fact. For those people who feel that entertainment is an integral part of selling, we cite our findings in the Dallas study. The saleswomen reported that they had no need to entertain their prospective buyers. The one saleswoman who did any entertaining at all always did so with her sales manager present. Industrial saleswomen are proving that you don't have to wine and dine customers to sell them goods. Company treasurers are going to be very happy to learn of this discovery, not to mention the stockholders.

Myth Seven—*The Good Salesperson Never Takes No for an Answer*
There isn't a salesperson alive who sells to everyone. People will turn your proposition down—and rightly so

if it is wrong for them. Other times there will be people who are not prospects for your goods. These people don't need your product or cannot afford it. Don't feel you failed when someone says no to you.

In retailing, remember that the person who declines to buy today will be back another day to buy something else if you handle the situation correctly. But if you are so aggressive in trying to make an immediate sale that the shopper is ill at ease, that person is unlikely to return. People do not want to be pressured, and they avoid places where they expect to feel it.

This is not to say that there aren't people who need your product and can well afford it but who say no as a matter of habit. They hate to spend money. It is in dealing with these people that the skilled salesperson is needed to turn those nos into yeses.

Myth Eight—*The Locker Room Syndrome*
Many people think that the successful industrial salesperson does most of his business on the golf course, at ball games, and around the poker table. The image of the hard-drinking, sports-loving, poker-playing male chauvinist has permeated the sales world for years. Well, the women in our Dallas survey dispelled this myth. They felt no disadvantage at being unable to participate in the male locker room ritual. They felt no need to play golf or poker with customers or to go to ball games with them. They simply sold their products to people who needed them. Now isn't that a quaint way to do business?

Myth Nine—*Selling Is a Bag of Tricks*
True, there are sales techniques, but success is not merely a matter of mastering them. Take any one sales

technique. Some people will use it successfully; others will not.

The technique does not determine success. You, the salesperson, do that—for it is your own experience that will teach you which techniques work for you.

Myth Ten—*People Don't Want to Buy*
Many sales managers are guilty of espousing the idea that people don't want to buy merchandise and, therefore, you as salesperson must beat them over the head and twist their arms to get the order. If people didn't want to buy merchandise, the majority of salespeople would be starving. A very low percentage of the goods and services purchased results from the creative selling efforts of salespeople. Most goods are bought because people want them. People want new cars, nice houses, new dresses, shoes, or whatever. They want all sorts of things. This is particularly true of industrial buyers who must buy all the things that their companies need for operations—they must buy! They are waiting for the salesperson to show them how his or her proposition is going to benefit them. They have the money and the desires. It's the salesperson's job to get together with them.

Myth Eleven—*The "Quick Riches" Illusion*
Selling is not an easy profession that you can master quickly and see financial gain immediately. Experience provides many lessons; nowhere is this so evident as in selling. The experienced salesperson has developed ways and accumulated knowledge that the beginner cannot begin to appreciate. The experienced salesperson can readily recall numerous instances that parallel the prospect's situation and can be used as effective persuaders. The beginner lacks such a background. The

veteran has a reliable clientele; the beginner has none. Do not expect immediate success in sales. If you are, more to your credit. But if you are not, do not be discouraged, because your expectations are unrealistic. It will take time for you to hone your selling skills to find out what works for you.

What is a salesperson...

A "salesperson" sells a product or service to someone who needs it and can afford to pay for it. This professional person spends a lot of time trying to find people who need the product. When such a prospect is found, the industrial salesrep spends considerable time studying the situation to determine how to best serve the prospective customer—that is, he or she develops solutions to the customer's problems.

What Is Selling?

Selling is a matter of pinpointing problems and then devising solutions for them.

Selling is the delivering of benefits, not products. Customers don't buy products; they buy what the products can do for them. People buy quarter-inch holes, not quarter-inch drill bits.

Selling is seeing the people. There's no substitute for getting out and calling on accounts. You must contact them, either in person or by telephone, although admittedly in some fortuitous circumstances loyal customers will send orders to you.

Selling is setting up annuities. An annuity, once purchased, pays off regularly thereafter. The truly professional industrial salesperson when calling on an industrial account isn't interested so much in the first order received as in all future orders from that account. You're playing a game with much larger stakes than most people can imagine. When you have a large industrial account as a customer, you have an annuity that will pay off month after month, year after year if you properly service and take care of that account. Thus the professional salesrep is not interested in making the first sale at all costs; rather he or she wants to gain all the customer's business for the future. Consequently, selling is the delivery of continued satisfaction to the customer, which places great stress on the servicing aspects of selling. Once you have a customer, you must make sure the account is given the best service possible. As a result, the customer and the industrial salesperson become good friends. They do not have the dog-and-cat adversary relationship so often pictured. After all, why wouldn't somebody like someone who is giving them excellent service?

Some Basic Philosophies

Many people fail in selling because of their attitudes—their philosophies. One study of the people who failed in life insurance selling indicated that one important factor in the failure pattern was guilt. The agents felt guilty about invading the privacy of the people they were calling on. This guilt ultimately caused their failure, because people are reluctant to do something continually about which they feel guilty.

Others failed because they simply did not believe in life insurance. Not believing in the product, how could they recommend it with the necessary sincerity and enthusiasm? From the study we gather two essential philosophies for success in selling. First, believe in your product. You must believe that it is the best product for the money on the market. If you do not have the utmost confidence in the goods you sell, then go to work for a firm in whose products you do have confidence. The selling job is such that unless you believe in what you're doing, you won't do it with conviction. Few people are such consummate liars that they can fool prospects repeatedly.

Second, sell to people who need your product. When you leave after making a sale, you should be able to say truthfully to yourself that the buyer is better off for having bought from you. If you have the slightest thought that you had best get out the door before the customer wises up to the fact that he's been flimflammed, then you had best change jobs because you are not a salesperson, you're a crook.

Self-Confidence

Self-confidence has been one of the major stumbling blocks keeping women from going into industrial selling. In nearly every instance in which a woman failed to succeed in sales work, as disclosed in our Dallas survey, the reason given was the individual's lack of self-confidence.

Saleswoman—Business Systems

I feel I've grown in self-confidence tremendously this year. As an example of what I mean, I recall the time my husband and I were looking for a place for the rehearsal dinner for our wedding. The restaurant we were interested in was closed; so I said to my husband, 'Let's walk around the back.' He said we couldn't do that, but I told him we'd just walk in the back door. The worst thing they can do is throw us out. We walked in the back door and were ushered into the chef's office. We told the chef our price limit for what we wanted. Bob was stunned. We got a lovely dinner within the price limit. For the hour we were there, the chef rolled out the red carpet.

I'm much more confident than I used to be. Last year when I started out as a saleswoman I was hesitant and not sure of myself. I kept asking myself, "Can I really do that?" Now I know I can do it.

Self-confidence is a complex set of concepts. There are many other terms used more or less synonymously and in conjunction with it. Self-assurance is certainly a close relative. There's the canard about the salesperson whom other people called cocky, but she preferred to think of herself as self-confident. Certainly, the self-assured person can often project an air of cockiness, but she need not do so.

Certainly, people are not born with self-confidence; that is, it's not an innate trait. Nothing in our genes predetermines our self-confidence, which is behavior learned through experience. We become self-confident as we learn we can do things. We become self-confident when we learn we have the ability to learn to do things. We are self-confident when we have learned not to be fearful of any situation, for we have learned that we can handle it. As one very successful professional salesrep bragged, "I've been around for a number of years now, long enough to know that I can whip anything that walks through the door. I fear nothing."

The man speaking is not referring to physical violence. He is simply saying he feels able to handle any problem he encounters. He has confidence in his ability to cope.

Explaining in depth how he got his self-confidence, the man said, "In thinking back, I developed confidence in my abilities when I was in high school. When I was a sophomore trying to make the basketball team, I was sitting on the sidelines and saw how much the coaches liked rough play. They liked the guys who were able to come off the board with the ball. They didn't much care how you got the ball as long as you got it. So the next time in a practice game I went all out to get the ball. Every time it went up in the air I came down with it, and I was a bit rough on a few teammates doing it. Out of the corner of my eye I saw the coaches jumping up and down pointing at me. It wasn't just coincidence that I started the next game. I was proud of myself because I had been able to analyze the situation and figure out what I had to do to get what I wanted. I wanted to be on the first team. I figured out what the coach wanted and did it. And you know ever since then I have been able to figure out what it takes to do a job and do it. Oh, every now and then, of course, I lose. You can't win them all. But I certainly don't lose for lack of self-confidence. And I never lose for fear of failing."

This last remark brings up another aspect that relates to self-confidence: the fear of failure. Many people never succeed because they fear failure. The threat of failure is your greatest enemy. Oh, it's easy to put a finger on why we're afraid to fail. No one wants to be looked on as a failure or to have people whispering behind your back, laughing at you, "Ha, ha, Mary fell on her face" or something similar. People are quick to pounce on the failures of others, but the successful individual pays no attention to such talk knowing that most of these people are jealous losers who eagerly point to other people's failures to lessen the pain of their own failures. One truth the successful person has discovered is that you'll never succeed at anything if you're afraid to fail. Moreover, you'll never learn much unless you do fail. Many people have failed dismally in business. Yet from the lessons learned in failure they forged successful careers. Everyone makes mistakes, but the successful person learns from his or her mistakes.

Thus I feel that the person who wants to gain confidence and self-assurance must experience failure. You must expose yourself to failure. Expose yourself to a chance to learn, and you can be certain that one of your learning experiences will be that failure doesn't really hurt much. The fact that somebody tells you to get out of the office doesn't hurt. It's only your opinion of this act hurting you that it does or does not. The professional salesperson thinks, "OK, stay ignorant and lose the benefits of my product." The even more professional salesperson thinks, "It appears I've made a mistake. Now where did I go wrong?"

One of the problems involved with our fear of failure is that we are overly concerned with what other people think of us. We want other people to like us and think well of us. We want it too much for our own good. We do too many things just to affect other people's opinions of us. Successful people will tell you that on their way to the top they encountered jealous "friends" and acquaintances who tried to hurt them. But they had to learn not to live their lives to placate others.

Self-confidence. What is it? Self-confidence is an inner belief in one's ability, self-worth, and importance as a human being. No one is born with self-confidence. Hopefully, it is a trait that is nurtured, beginning in early childhood. The baby is encouraged to respond, urged to walk, coaxed to talk, and praised lavishly for the first unsure words and faltering steps. Each accomplishment and its effect increases the baby's self-confidence.

Self-confidence is no more a feeling of superiority than it is one of inferiority. It is the ingredient that results in self-assurance and the unspoken conviction that one can deal successfully with life and its challenges. No one is confident at all times. The more confident you are, however, the more you are in control of your life and destiny. Confident people are able to project their feelings toward others and others respond accordingly. People often mistake the blustering overbearing individual as being self-confident. The loud egotist is often tremendously insecure. Self-confidence results in inner strength. When you have self-confidence you can make decisions, sense when you are right, and stand by your convictions. The confident person can deal with the consequences of failure and is not threatened or unduly influenced by others. This individual does not suffer the pangs of jealousy so often felt by the insecure.

Society is not always conducive to your self-confidence. We live in a highly mechanized age. Our children do not have the advantage of seeing how the food they eat, the clothing they wear, and the income enjoyed by the family are produced. We live in a huge and bewildering world. It is harder than ever to raise our children to be sufficient. Commonly, children are greatly influenced by television which by its very nature encourages the child to become passive instead of an active participant in life. Schools in the major cities are so large that athletic teams do not rely on their entire classes for support. It is difficult for today's child to receive individual recognition and attention.

Everyone needs some recognition—some glory. But achieving glory can be difficult in today's mass world. In my high school class of 60 youngsters glory was easy to come by—just do something. There weren't enough bodies around to claim all the available glory. Today, I am fond of asking students, "What's your road to glory?" For a while the question puzzles them, but later they say the ensuing discussion opens up new doors for them. Everybody needs some glory. Learn to provide it and you'll go far.

Competition is fierce and the child often finds it simpler not to compete at all. We parents can be extreme in our instinctual wish to shelter our children from the harsh reality of life. We seldom realize that in doing so we may actually cripple the child's ability to cope with life's challenges.

Is it more difficult for a woman to gain self-confidence than a man?

By participating more fully in life's activities—work, sports, and politics, today's women have gained self-confidence. The older woman, a product of an earlier era, may find it more difficult to become self-confident than the male. This woman's childhood took place in a setting influenced by tradition. Typically, she was reared to be noncompetitive, passive, and supportive. Asserting herself does not come easy. She was probably reared with a definite image to live up to— the feminine ideal. Little boys were encouraged to work in teams, to cooperate, to be strong, to make decisions, and to stand up for themselves. Little girls were encouraged to play out roles in which they were little mommies, they were supportive, and it was acceptable for them to run away and cry when things became unpleasant.

Today's woman finds herself in a rapidly changing society in which women play an increasingly

*important role in the national work force. She finds
that she is pulled in opposite directions. The
traditional influences that shaped her and surround
her pull in one direction and the current progressive
demands and ideas pull her in another direction.*

*When a woman begins a career in selling she must
make a commitment that she is willing to risk
rejection and failure. Then she takes her training and
product out to obtain a sales order. A signed sales
contract is a great boost to one's self-confidence. The
woman has the satisfaction of realizing that her
efforts and abilities have resulted in dollars and
benefits for herself, her company, and her client.
I have noticed a change that occurs in a room
immediately following the signing of a contract. Up
until the crucial moment, there has usually been an
air of intense concentration. There have been
penetrating questions and some serious and lengthy
deliberation. Once the contract is signed, however,
there usually is a change of mood. The atmosphere
clears. Spirits lift and the buyer seems happy, often
even relieved. The attitude the buyer projects toward
the salesperson becomes personal and confidential. He
or she seems to regard the salesperson as a friend. An
air of trust has been established. A decision has been
made. The salesperson has the satisfaction of knowing
that she has influenced the buyer in a positive
direction. After exposing herself to rejection and
putting her ego on the line, she has impressed the
buyer to the point where he or she is willing to invest
money in the salesrep's product and consequently in
her. She has successfully put a cycle into motion. She
realizes that this initial order can be the first of many.*

She begins to realize that her financial gain will be determined by the effort she is willing to extend and she can see she is a powerful person in her own right. She has just placed a building block firmly in the foundation of her self-confidence.

One other factor in gaining self-confidence is that when there is something you want to do, you accept that you can do it. You accept that you can make it happen. And making this happen brings us to mental toughness, a subject discussed in depth later.

What kind of sales job is for you . . .

As is true in other professions, your success in selling depends to a large extent on how well you and your job are suited for one another. Management, of course, is most interested in whether you will be able to get the job done. Sales management literature dwells on the task of eliciting from you sufficient background information so that a judgment can be made on your likelihood of satisfying the job's requirements.

But there is another side to it. While it is important from your personal viewpoint that you and the sales manager determine whether you can do the job successfully, it is also important to both of you to determine if the job satisfies your specifications. Can you get what you need from it? The following factors are not presented in order of importance, an impossibility, because the significance of each depends entirely on your situation and attitudes.

Home and Family Restraints

Our study of industrial saleswomen indicated that women were particularly sensitive to the demands placed on them by their families. Many of the women relish their sales positions because the flexibility of the jobs allowed them to satisfy the demands placed on them at home.

Saleswoman—Microfilm Equipment

I think instead of a woman just hopping into any sales job she should take time to study the products to be sold and how they are marketed. I wouldn't be able to fit into certain markets because I have children. I'd love to travel, but I have a conflict; so I studied what kinds of jobs had no travel requirements. I want zero travel. . . . I wanted a job that would give me a car and expenses. Why not?

This ability to meet the irregular demands of one's family is one of the big advantages offered by industrial sales positions. When an emergency arises at home, the industrial saleswoman usually can adjust her call schedule to handle the situation.

In the traditional male world it was axiomatic that the man who hoped for success had to have a home situation that placed few, if any, constraints on his dedication to the business. Business folklore reported that the man had to be able to travel at will, spend whatever nights at work that were required, and did not have to cater to the demands of a whining wife.

But there are whining husbands who place demands on the business woman. And the children have been brought up to run to momma on the slightest whim. Thus the married industrial saleswoman may not feel able to assume the stance taken by the previous male model who expected the family to place a minimum of demands on him.

Consequently, industrial saleswoman must realistically appraise the demands that will be made on her by her family and find a sales job to accommodate them. The woman with school-aged children may likely take a different type of selling job than a woman with no

children at home. The single woman, of course, is
allowed far more freedom in the job she selects.

Pay Demands

Of course pay is important. Any person who tells you
otherwise is either an fool or is trying to hire you. It
should come as no surprise to you to learn that jobs vary
greatly in what they pay, both in the amount of earnings
that you can anticipate and their regularity.

One of the hallmarks of many industrial sales jobs is
that they pay straight commission; thus earnings can
fluctuate, sometimes greatly, depending on business
conditions. If your home situation and financial capability demand a certain minimum income each month,
then the sales job you accept should be able to provide
it. You'll have to avoid the feast-and-famine jobs.

There are many excellent industrial sales jobs, particularly those that involve selling large equipment and
expensive installations, where you might make only one
or two sales a year, but they are of such size that your
earnings can be quite handsome. However, you must be
able to finance yourself over the dry periods. One of the
distinct advantages of industrial saleswomen who have
husbands with well-paying jobs is that these women can
take sales jobs in which earnings, while most satisfactory in total, are nevertheless unstable. When the family
is not counting on a monthly paycheck, the industrial
saleswoman has more freedom to aim as high as she
can.

Of course, the level of pay is critical. Some sales jobs
pay handsomely; others pay modestly. The level of pay
varies substantially in the same industry. To women,
one of the attractions of industrial selling is that generally, they can earn more money than they can in other

jobs, considering background qualifications. This is particularly true of industrial salespeople paid on a straight commission basis.

You should have clearly in mind how much a year you expect to earn from the sales job before you ever accept it. But do be realistic. Unrealistic expectations, particularly in the early years, leads to unnecessary disillusionment. You'll not likely get rich quick in any job of which we know.

What is the range of earnings that can be expected? Naturally, precise data about industrial saleswomen's earnings are not available. All we have are some opinions of people whose positions qualify them to speak on the matter. David King, founder of Careers for Women, a marketing school for women, stated, "If you are average, you'll earn $25,000 a year by the time you're finished with the first three years of your selling career. Many of you can be earning $40,000 and $50,000 a year after five or six years' experience."*

We think David King is fair in his estimates. Naturally, in such estimates, what is being sold is important. Some sales jobs pay as much as he states; others pay far more.

Travel Constraints

Some people don't like to travel; others are unable to. But there are people who enjoy traveling and consider it definitely a positive attribute of some industrial sales jobs. Now understand that most industrial selling jobs require a bit of driving around a metropolitan area. Few salespeople work strictly in an office. And some

---

*David King and Karen Levine, "Yes, you can! make $50,000 a year," *Family Circle*, May 15, 1979, p. 58.

industrial sales jobs require some nights away from home. Normally, this is not a difficult decision for you to make because you know the constraints placed on you by your personal situation. Sometimes people initially feel that traveling would be an interesting experience, but they often find that after a few months on the road it just becomes an experience. All the industrial saleswomen interviewed in the Dallas survey incurred no problems in managing the amount of travel required by their jobs. Most were home as much as they wanted to be.

Indeed, one woman reported that her favorite escape tactic when things were getting to her around home was to get in the car and cover some of the outlying cities in her territory for a day or so.

Saleswoman—Business Equipment
I wouldn't want a sales job where I was gone Monday through Friday, because I've got so many activities in the community. I wouldn't want to spend my life in a hotel room. That's why this job is so perfect for me: I don't have to travel.

Sales Manager—Pharmaceutical Company
I would be very reluctant to hire a woman and put her out, for instance, in the Midland-Odessa area. It's rather sparse there, and there are certain risks. I don't think it's fair for the woman to be on the road spending maybe two or three nights a week away from home. I get really worried. There's a lot of screwballs out there. I place women in a metro area.

With women entering sales in increasing numbers, it's understandable that many are finding themselves in positions in which they are required to travel. For many women this represents a whole new frontier that can appear not only exciting, but also frightening.

*What are the advantages and the disadvantages for
the woman who suddenly finds herself in this
position? Is she looked on with distaste by her male
travelers? Is she treated badly? Do men assume that
she is a pickup if she has a drink in a hotel lounge
before dinner?*

*According to one single woman who is also a single
mother and who has traveled extensively, traveling for
the woman is exactly what she makes of it.*

Case

Vicki was an account manager for Revlon's top line, Borghese. She
traveled three weeks out of every month. She quit because she felt it was
unfair to her child to be away from home that much. She does not advise
travel for a woman with responsibilities at home.

"A woman is treated in a manner that she controls and projects," Vicki
states frankly.

"Women must accept the fact that they are living in a world where there
is a double standard and act accordingly. If she gets drunk in a hotel
lounge or in a flight between calls she will be looked on with disapproval
and she will not be accorded respect. On the other hand, it seems quite
ordinary when a businessman has one too many martinis. The circumstances may be the same, but the reaction of others is decidedly different.
If a woman conducts herself like a lady she will be treated as such."

Vicki is polished, sophisticated, attractive, and extremely knowledgeable
in her field. Having traveled for years, she states that most of the men she
encountered while traveling were courteous and eager to assist her in
any problems that might arise. When she took her first flight to call on a
department store in Atlanta, she was very nervous. The fact that no one
would be at the airport to meet her added to her uneasiness. However,
everything went smoothly, and traveling soon became routine. She said
that it is normal for novices to be nervous until they have mastered the
skills of the experienced traveler. Airline schedules and hotel reservations
frighten the beginner.

One of Vicki's biggest irritations was that the man sitting next to her on a
plane would likely try to engage her in a conversation. Sometimes this
was fine, but other times she needed to do paperwork or was just too
tired to want to talk to anyone.

"You do get hustled," she states calmly. "At first this took me back a bit, but I learned quickly to say things such as 'I'm sorry. I'm seriously involved with someone' or 'I just can't talk right now. I'm involved in this proposal and am limited for time' or 'I'm just exhausted; do you mind if I close my eyes and try to catch a nap before we land?'"

Vicki claims that many of the older men took a fatherly and protective attitude toward her, expressing admiration toward her ability to handle both the responsibility of the job and that of being a parent. Once a mix-up occurred regarding her hotel reservations. The hotel was full, but a man checking in at the same time, who had been on her flight, insisted on her taking his hotel room.

Only once did she find herself in an uncomfortable position. She met an attractive, distinguished looking man in a hotel lobby while checking in late one afternoon. They had been on the same flight and he invited her to join him for dinner in the hotel's dining room. Vicki accepted. At first he was a perfect gentleman, but as the evening proceeded he had too much to drink. He became increasingly overbearing and verbally crude. Finally, the situation became so uncomfortable that Vicki arose without a word and went directly to her room. A short time later the man, now quite drunk, began pounding on her door, demanding that she come out and talk. She told him in no uncertain terms that if he did not leave immediately she would call the hotel manager to register a complaint. He left and to her relief she never saw him again. Vicki feels that simple precautions can save a woman a lot of problems while traveling. She never gave out her hotel room number, always made sure no one was standing near her door when she entered, and observed the hallway carefully on leaving and entering. She made it a point to never meet a stranger in a lonely or deserted area.

Vicki feels that there is nothing wrong with a woman having a drink before dinner in a hotel lounge or accepting an invitation for a drink and dinner by a man she meets in the hotel. If the man makes the wrong assumption, she believes that is his problem. She repeats her advice that a woman who conducts herself properly and with dignity will be treated in a like manner except in a few instances.

Many of the problems Vicki encountered while traveling were problems that both men and women shared. As she explains, "Often I would put in a fourteen-hour day, but only four to six had been spent in an actual sales meeting. An enormous amount of time is required in securing hotel reservations, flight times, and actual travel. Dealing with this cuts down on an individual's efficiency and can be extremely exhausting."

Vicki points out that traveling is very lonely and becomes monotonous. Sleeping in hotel rooms and eating in restaurants quickly becomes a grind.

The firm Vicki worked for did its best to make her job secure. Vicki was encouraged to stay at the best hotels and had a generous expense account. She was furnished a company car and the fringe benefits were excellent. Her base salary was $15,000 yearly, with a yearly bonus never less than $5,000.

The only criticism Vicki expressed of the company was that her territory was so big and her duties so numerous that she was unable to do justice to anything. She believes that more was expected of her as a woman than would have been expected of a man in her position. "We [the women reps] did more for our customers than the male reps and I suspect we were paid less. I never saw a man work behind a makeup counter or give makeup demonstrations, but we were expected to do such work if the store was shorthanded."

While Vicki felt her job was excellent, her personal responsibilities forced her to quit. The company offered her a substantial raise to stay, but she had made her decision. She is now a cosmetics buyer for a department store.

Educational Restraints

What are your educational and intellectual capabilities? Many industrial sales jobs require considerable engineering knowledge. If you have never relished the technical arts, you had better select a sales job not requiring them.

On the other hand, don't automatically reject a job because you're afraid you don't know enough to do it. Many companies furnish excellent sales training programs that will provide the technical knowledge you'll need. All that's required is the requisite intelligence and the desire to master the material.

Your Threshold of Boredom

Many routine sales jobs are boring. You must sell the same mundane products to the same people who talk about the same things day in and day out. There may be little challenge to the job. You do little more than deliver the milk. Some people thrive on such jobs while others flee from them.

This examination of the tasks of a middled-aged woman working as a housewares rack-jobber shows that boredom is relative to the individual. This woman stocks the supermarket's shelves with the housewares handled by her boss.

The rack-jobber is a wholesaler who places goods into a store on consignment and who, therefore, is totally responsible for maintaining the stock in the store. The store gets a percentage on the goods sold. Now, restocking supermarket shelves with housewares is not considered one of the more challenging industrial sales jobs. But this woman is perfectly happy doing it, considering it a vast improvement over her previous job on a factory assembly line.

Of course many industrial sales jobs exist that are anything but boring. You meet many interesting people and the problems encountered are endlessly varying and truly challenging.

An advertising space saleswoman reported that what she enjoyed most about her job was the creative challenge of having to help small businesses develop effective, but modest, advertising programs in her magazine.

Personal Goals

People have personal goals they want to accomplish. Perhaps you want to earn a certain amount of money. Perhaps you want job security. Perhaps power attracts you. Some people seek status and will only work where this is attainable. What is it you want? Once you figure this out, you'll have to determine whether the job you are contemplating will furnish it. If you cannot achieve your personal goals through the job being offered, you might be wise to look elsewhere, because sooner or later the inability of that job to give you what you want will cause you problems. Either you'll become dissatisfied and your morale will sag, or you'll quit.

Case

Kim wanted to have her own womenswear shop, but instead accepted a job with a large department store as a management trainee. Exceptionally talented, she was made manager of a large sportwear department at a significant shopping mall branch store. But this was not what she wanted and it quickly got to her. She had to be her own boss and the sooner the better.

If a job won't allow you to reach your goals, you'll not likely be happy with it.

Nature of the Job

The nature of the products you are selling may be repugnant or distasteful to you. If so, don't take the job. Experience clearly shows that the people most successful in selling are those who enjoy dealing with the products they sell. One young woman who was selling for a pharmaceutical company was not overly enchanted with calling on physicians, but she did enjoy the drug business and the technical aspects of what she was learning and doing. The nature of the industry overall was sufficient to make the young woman put aside her particular distaste for calling on physicians.

Additionally, it helps if you like the people you deal with. A saleswoman for Spalding golf equipment reported difficulty breaking into that traditionally male world, but she enjoys golf and the people involved in golf so much that she considers it worthwhile to try this field of sales.

Personal Freedom

How much personal freedom do you require? In some sales jobs you will work very closely under a supervisor who directs you each day to call on certain accounts. You will have very little personal freedom. In other sales jobs, you are given a sales territory and from there on you are only responsible for meeting your sales quotas. You are almost totally free to manage that territory as you wish, working when you want to and calling on those you think it would be best to call on.

While it might seem obvious that everyone would like a great deal of freedom, such is not the case. Many people are absolutely horrified by the thought that they are totally responsible for deciding what they are to do. They want to be told what to do. They prosper in a highly structured situation. This is not surprising if one recalls that we carefully regiment our young people through 12 and perhaps 16 years of highly structured educational experiences in which they are told, almost each minute of the day, exactly where to be and what to do. Those unwilling to accept such regimentation are drummed out of the educational system as malcontents, troublemakers, incorrigibles, or worse. Public school systems insist on regimentation. Is it any surprise that the graduates of our educational system are unable to accommodate highly unstructured, ambiguous environments in which they're free to do a great number of things? Suddenly, no one is there to tell them what to do. I have seen salespeople emotionally destroyed by having such tremendous responsibility suddenly placed on them. These people want managements that will again place them in a highly structured environment and tell them precisely what to do and when to do it. But this is not selling.

How well can you operate in an unstructured, ambiguous situation? "Ambiguous" means that the world is continually feeding you conflicting, confused clues about what it wants you to do. What behavior is expected of you? You just can't get a clear reading on what path to take and what to do at all times. Some people just can't handle ambiguous environments. Yet the world is ambiguous, particularly the business world. Naturally, to be successful in it you must be able to cope with the ambiguities and understand that such is normal. Everything isn't logical. Everything does not work by the numbers.

The highly successful industrial salesperson is normally one who prospers in ambiguous situations. He or she looks on ambiguous situations as opportunities rather than as inhibitive factors.

Relationship with Superiors

In some sales jobs you will work closely with superiors; in others, you will seldom see them. As mentioned earlier, some people work well without supervision, others are unable to manage their time. How much supervision do you need? The Dallas study uniformly disclosed that the women felt they needed more supervision and help than they were getting. This was natural considering their limited sales experience. They were pioneering. Largely, they were not experienced in sales. They lacked confidence. Thus it is only natural that from such a background there would be a great need for supervision.

As part of their relationship with superiors, some employees expect their bosses to be father figures or perhaps big brothers. And some bosses are perfectly willing to play these roles. And there are women bosses who play the role of mother or big sister. On the other hand, some managers have no desires to play such roles. They see their jobs almost solely in terms of business and its requirements.

In a further extension of the employee/superior relationship, it's not uncommon in a relatively small sales office for a family-like environment to develop, projecting a "we're all one big happy family" atmosphere. Many management theorists have criticized such attitudes and point out unfortunate consequences of them, but on the other hand there is a lot to say for the idea. Perhaps the Japanese industrial experience will cause some management experts to reconsider their attitudes toward such paternalism. The Japanese industrial structure is highly paternalistic and also highly successful. (Some people, both men and women, prosper and flourish in such social settings. They want to be a member of the family.)

There are many people who look forward to work because they enjoy their "home at work" more than they enjoy their home in the suburbs. Think about it. At work there are no children screaming at you, no spouses making unreasonable demands, and when the plumbing doesn't work, it's someone else's problem.

Need for Training

How much training do you need? If you are just starting in the industrial sales world, be assured that you need a great deal of training. You should only consider accepting a job with an employer who is willing to give you that training and who is patient enough to wait until you're ready before placing you on the firing line.

Mobility

One of the problems most written about in our new culture concerning the lives of the two-breadwinner families is the matter of job transfers. Historically, the woman has followed the man wherever his job took him. But that day is ending. More and more the wife's career is every bit as important, if not more so, than the man's. The woman often has an excellent job and if the husband is transferred it would force the woman to leave that good job and, in all probability, get a lesser one. Her own company cannot or will not arrange a transfer of convenience.

More and more large companies are going to have to modify their transfer policies to accommodate this new cultural attribute. If they want to hire people whose spouses also have meaningful careers, they're going to have to take the career of the spouses into consideration in their transfer policies.

If your husband is likely to be transferred, and normally you know the policies of his employer, you might want to consider working for a company whose policies can accommodate transfers. This would mean you would want to go to work for a nationwide company with sales offices in all areas so that there would be a high likelihood you could work for the company wherever your husband would be transferred. You should probe into this matter with the potential employer early in negotiations.

One reason you do not want to change locales and employers in industrial selling is that the longer you work for one company in one industry calling on one set of customers, the more successful you will be. It takes months and sometimes years to build a clientele in a territory. After a number of years with one concern, you get to know the trade and territory and this is reflected handsomely in your productivity. To just pull up and move to a new area may well destroy the continuity that is so important in industrial selling. Thus it is a great value to you if you can stay in one area.

What to look for in an industrial sales job . . .

By now, it should be clear that all sales jobs are not equally attractive. Consequently, you should have clearly in mind some expectations when evaluating a prospective sales position.

Training Program

One of the earmarks of such excellent industrial sales forces as IBM, Xerox, and Armstrong Cork is their ongoing top-flight sales training programs. These firms do a fine job of training people how to sell. Naturally, it costs a great deal of money to maintain such training programs, but these firms have found that such expenditures are worthwhile, for they pay off handsomely in sales force productivity.

To develop an effective sales training program, it takes considerable experience and know-how, not to mention a dedicated management. Many firms have neither the inclination nor talent for accomplishing such. Indeed, it is the strategy of a large number of concerns to let the big companies—IBM and Xerox—

do their training for them. Then these firms simply recruit their salespeople from those firms with excellent training programs. At one time in the textbook publishing field Prentice-Hall was widely reknowned for the excellence of its sales training program. It is not surprising, therefore, that many top executives in all publishing houses today started their careers with Prentice-Hall, because at that time it was the only company doing much of what could be considered sales training. The other firms simply pirated Prentice-Hall's personnel.

You need training. Thus look for an employer who offers an effective sales training program. Do not be misled for one instant when some eager sales manager waxes ebulliently over the two-week training program he is going to put you through. Likely, you will not learn how to be a successful saleswoman in two weeks. In relation to the training provided, you should be interested in the continual training and supervision you will be given during the first year of employment. Make up your mind right now that it's going to take some time for you to develop into a highly productive salesperson. While some cases exist of highly motivated women who have become tremendously successful largely on their own endeavors, it's much easier and more effective when management can provide you some help along the way. That's one of the reasons for management. Good management develops its people. Thus when you see a management that is not oriented toward developing these skills you're not looking at very good management.

This doesn't mean you must work for one of the large corporations that maintains a formal sales training program. But unfortunately, such does preclude your going to work in many attractive positions in smaller concerns. After all, a small concern may have only one salesperson. So it cannot afford to establish a formal training program. In such instances, you need to probe into the sales manager's realization that he or someone in the organization must be devoted to your training and development.

You should ask some pointed questions during the job interview such as, "How much training will I receive and who will do it?" And do get explanations. You'll be surprised how many employers haven't given much thought to the matter. The training such employers offer will be on a hit-or-miss basis, and this usually means miss, not hit.

Office Support

In many concerns, salespeople are put into a territory and from there on they are on their own. They receive little support from the home office. Home office support is a multitude of little, but important, things. For example, you're calling on a customer and something out of the ordinary comes up and you need some information or a quotation that you don't have (this happens frequently in industrial selling). You need help quickly. In well-managed concerns there is someone you can telephone directly at the home office to immediately get the help you need to make the sale. In many concerns you have difficulty getting the needed information or it might be several days or even weeks during which the customer gives the order to some other concern. Thus prompt, excellent home office technical support is a great sales help.

You get the order and send it in for processing marked RUSH because the customer badly needs the goods. What happens to the order in the home office? Is it processed as quickly as possible? Are the orders expedited? Just how well does management back up your sales efforts? You will find it most embarrassing, and detrimental to your career, when you promise your customer delivery in a week and the goods get there in two weeks. Deliveries are often critical in industrial selling. It will be most beneficial to your career to work for firms that are able to give excellent service to their customers. While you might be tempted to think that your goal as an industrial saleswoman is to get the order, actually the order is only the first step. The goal is to satisfy the customer and this is not achieved until the goods are in the house and are being used satisfactorily. Unless this happens you will not get another order from that customer.

What happens if something goes wrong with the goods that are sold? From a marketing standpoint, and always bear in mind that as an industrial saleswoman you are but one cog in the marketing machine, the key to success in industrial selling is service. If a machine goes bad at a company you serve, you may have to go there immediately to fix the problem. Often large sums of money are at stake, depending on the promptness of your repair service. It will greatly increase your productivity to work for firms that deliver such top-notch service.

Compensation Plans

Pay is important. And it is important how it is paid.

The key factors you should look for are these: Is the company willing to pay off if you are successful? Will your pay be proportionate to your productivity after you get into full-scale production? This means some form of incentive plan—either a straight commission or some salary plan, plus a significant commission. You'll seldom make big money in selling working on a salary. Few managements will be willing to pay you a high salary because they can usually hire someone else as good as you are to work for a more modest salary. A few top-notch managements can administer a sales salary plan so that it will provide both excellent incentive and high earnings for top producers. But these firms are exceptions.

However, initially, you need some sort of a pay plan that can support you while you're learning to support yourself. Thus companies usually will pay you a maintenance salary for six months or a year or until you're able to pay your way. Often, if the choice is left to you, you can work on a salary basis until you feel you're ready to work on a commission.

One trap that some saleswomen have encountered is the timing of the pay. Often firms pay commissions after they receive the money from the customer. This may mean a delay of several months between the time you take the order and the time the customer actually pays. Such a lag in pay can be frustrating. Find out when you are to be paid.

Some firms hold the salesperson responsible for credit losses. If the customer doesn't pay, you don't get your commission. You should look into this, for it may mean you have to pay for the credit department's follies.

Transfer Policy

Transfers are important in many situations. We have previously examined your mobility in determining what kind of job you will take. Thus at the outset you should determine whether a company will transfer you if the need arose for you to go elsewhere. Moreover, if such a transfer were to be permitted for your convenience, find out what, if any, are your moving allowances. Obviously, when permitting a transfer for your convenience, management seldom sees much logic in paying for such a move. But everything is negotiable and the basis for the negotiation is just how badly they want to keep you, which rests solely on how good you are. That is, how much money do you make for them? After all, doesn't everything sooner or later come down to that? How much money do you make for your employers? The more you make for them, the more bargaining power you have.

Fellow Salespeople

Take a look at the people with whom you'll be working. Evaluate them not on whether you like them or they like you, for in many cases this doesn't matter since you won't be working closely with them. Instead, evaluate them on how well they like their jobs. How long have they been working for the employer? What's their morale? Answers to these two questions will tell you more about the company and its management than will almost anything else. People don't leave good jobs. Excellent, well-managed sales forces have very low turnover. When you see a sales force in which all the salespeople are relatively new and there are few old-timers around, watch out. It is strongly recommended that you spend some time talking with other salespeople for their evaluations of the situation.

Also you should try to find out how much other salespeople are earning. Naturally, in most cases, the salespeople themselves are not going to tell you. So it may take some effort to find out how they're prospering. But make the effort. Take a look at the cars they're driving. Drive by their houses. Look at how they dress and what they do. In other words, take a look at their standards of living. This should give you some idea of how much they're making. Are they prospering or not? If they aren't prospering, you will not be likely to prosper.

History

Try to find out the history of the company—when was it started and by whom? What's been the company's success? You want to work for a company that is making good money. The firm that is making good profits can be more generous with you. Those having a hard time of it will normally be stingy with their pay and fringe benefits. Go to work for people who are successful and are making money. The highly profitable firm tends to do things right. They will spend money on services and back-up support. They can afford to give you training. They can afford to do all the things that need to be done to be successful. Moreover, the profits a firm makes provides you with concrete proof of what the market thinks of that company's offerings.

Firm's Reputation with Customers

Talk to some of the firm's customers. What is the reputation of the company among the people it serves? You may hear such complaints as it sells bad merchandise, makes poor deliveries, and overprices its goods. If this is what customers are saying, then this is what you're going to hear when you call on them. Be aware that it's tough enough to sell without having such additional burdens.

Financial Stability

Many concerns are financially unstable. While they may have erected a suitable facade of financial capability, in fact, they may not have sufficient money with which to pay you on payday. It happens all too frequently. Salespeople have been asked to wait awhile to receive the money owed them simply because the company was short of cash and other obligations were more pressing. When management asks for a delay just what can you do? Your job's involved and their request is always so reasonable. Nevertheless, it is aggravating and most unfair. It has been known to happen that salespeople were left empty-handed when companies have unexpectedly gone into bankruptcy. We mention this so that you will be aware that these things do happen. Moreover, such failures tend to tarnish your own reputation. Down deep other employers will wonder just what role you played in the failure of your employer. Did the company fail because you failed to sell enough goods? It does one's reputation little good to be connected with a failing enterprise.

It is also particularly important that you be aware of this information because firms in the last stages of solvency often eagerly hire anyone who will come and sell for them in the hopes that somehow these new salespeople will save the day by going out and selling a lot of merchandise. Thus when someone is all too eager to hire you and fails to behave as a prudent management should, be careful, for this may be a warning that management is in trouble and is hiring anyone it can get. Most assuredly no good comes from such situations. The authors are not aware of any such concerns that have ever benefitted by such hiring tactics, but we are aware of many people who have been sucked into such situations.

Attitude of Superior

Betty Harragan, author of *Games Your Mother Never Taught You,* made a most valid major point in emphasizing the importance of your immediate superior. She insisted that women wanting a business career must understand that a business is essentially a military organization and the action is in the line. The sales force and the production people are operating personnel in the line organization and in the line you have a chain of command that runs from your immediate superior to that person's superior. And in the military your immediate superior has a very real life or death hold on you. Life can be most miserable if your superior has it in for you or is inept. Would you care to follow an inept second lieutenant into battle? Your chances of survival would be slim. Similarly, if you work for an inept sales manager your development will be stifled and your chances for success slim.

Betty Harragan urged everyone to have an interview with the person for whom they would be working. Make sure this person wants you to work for him or her. Little good will come if someone in top management forces someone down the line to hire you over their objections. A superior whose throat you have been rammed down may make matters difficult for you. When you interview your prospective superior, you should be able to answer such questions as "Does this person really want me to work for him or her? Is this person a fair individual? Is this person competent?"

Fringe Benefits

Historically, salespeople are heavily discriminated against in the matter of fringe benefits. While other people working for the company were considered employees and provided the usual fringe benefits such as insurance, retirement plans, and access to various club facilities, salespeople were often regarded as independent contractors, not employees. This has been changing, but still there is considerable holdover. Retirement and insurance programs are important. An expense account, even an honest one, is worth a great deal of money to you.

A company car is money in your pocket. You should find out in detail every amenity the company offers its salespeople, for these are meaningful.

Are There Other Women Already in the Sales Force?

Pioneers pay a price. If you are the first saleswoman to be hired—meaning you're the token woman—you will encounter a few problems initially. The organization will be uncertain about you. You will spend some time and effort just trying to justify your existence. However, if the company has already hired saleswomen, the way has been paved for you. In our Dallas study of industrial saleswomen, it was commonly reported by the first saleswomen in the organizations that they were initially met with some suspicions and mistrust.

Saleswoman—Copying Equipment

We have two women salesreps, one in Dallas and one in Houston. The woman in Houston had no sales experience at all; so they put her under their wings, which they like because they can control her. She's not really a threat to them, but they don't really respect her because she does well. They hover over her and baby her. Men like to try to do that because in their own way, they are able to put you in your place. And they're not even aware of being malicious. You have to set a certain profile that is conducive to working with men. I get along well working with men. I think they respect me and I think they also like me, but they don't ask me to do things that they wouldn't ask of someone else; in turn I don't ask them to do something for me because I'm a woman.

Without doubt, saleswomen have some uncomfortable moments. But women moving into sales organizations that had already had women salesreps reported no problems with their assimilation into the force. The question of concern is whether a given company has learned how to employ and use women in its sales force or will the company have to learn how to do such at your expense?

If you are going to be the first woman on the sales force, you had better be prepared for what you will meet. You should prepare management that it is going to have to make some effort to pave the way for you.

What is expected of you by your boss?

A cynic might cry, "That's easy, work hard and keep your nose clean." But there's more to it. It's not enough to work hard; you must also work "smart." Let's examine a few other dimensions to this matter of managerial expectations.

Follow Orders

Essentially, management expects you to follow orders. In her speeches on the adjustment of women to corporate hierarchies, author Betty Harragan, makes a big point of this. She maintains that many women, not understanding the military nature of business organizations, don't understand that the boss expects orders to be followed. But this doesn't mean blind obedience to the extent that you do things which are illegal or against company policy. Similarly, it doesn't mean that you must react without relevant questions. Certainly, if you have critical information relating to work the boss has ordered you to do that might make your carrying out the order unwise, most bosses will discuss the matter. If you have a sound reason for doing something other than what you have been told, you can make it known; most managers will defer if your reasons are sound. On the other hand, the manager may have information about which you are unfamiliar that may overrule your evaluation of the situation. In the end, you are best advised to follow orders. Indeed, in "management heaven" there is a special exalted place for subordinates for whom it was said, "They did what they were told to do." One of the quickest ways to ruin your career in an organization is to gain the reputation of being a renegade.

Company Loyalty

While many writers on management have observed that most companies are unrealistic in their expectations regarding the loyalty of their employees, still they do expect your loyalty above and beyond the paycheck. Loyalty manifests itself in many ways. It's an attitude. Company loyalty may mean there are times you must stick up for your employer even though you're not certain the employer is right. Company loyalty means using the company's products. If you work for Ford and drive a Chevy, be not surprised if your loyalty is questioned. Company loyalty may mean that when asked how you like working for the company you reply with great affirmative enthusiasm. Company loyalty may mean that you don't wash corporate linen in public. Loyalty means that you don't tell tales out of school; corporate secrets stay that way. Some managers will consider you disloyal if you take the initiative in seeking a job elsewhere. The instant management learns that you are contemplating another job you will likely find your relations with management strained unless, of course, they dearly want to keep you.

You may rightly tell some customer to buy a competitor's product because it better solves the customer's problems. Regardless of the long-run wisdom of your action, many bosses would consider it disloyal to the company. Most assuredly, it is advantageous to your career in a company to develop an image of being loyal to it.

On the other hand, many observers of the managerial scene point out that there are millions of loyal company employees who have little to show for it. They would say that while it is important to appear to be loyal, actual dedicated loyalty does not insure success in the company.

Company Policy

Successful careers in large organizations depend on one's ability never to be caught making a serious mistake outside of company policy. As long as your actions are within corporate policy you have a marvelous shield from condemnation by superiors: "I was just following policy in the matter." But do something outside of policy and you jeopardize your career. Even if your action is clearly successful, you still may be shocked to find yourself subjected to criticism from higher-ups: "I know it worked, but it was against company policy; so don't do it again." If the results of your action were disastrous and you were outside company policy, you may be looking for a job elsewhere, with the reasoning: "We told you not to do it; it was against policy."

You must understand that company policies are the same as orders. They are standing orders from higher-ups on the decisions that must be made regarding policy-related matters. When you go against policy you are disobeying orders.

Territorial Responsibility

In many industrial sales situations you are given a carefully delineated territory in which the responsibility for selling a certain line of products is yours alone. The company has placed in your hands the responsibility for its most valuable assets—its customers. This is a very serious responsibility. If you mess up the territory or alienate the customers, the company will likely pay severely for it in years to come. The customers must be serviced properly. It is your responsibility to do it. Strangely, some salespeople fail to comprehend the seriousness of this. When a customer calls to complain that something has gone wrong, some salespeople don't seem to know that the customer is demanding immediate rectification of the error. The customer wants something done and is not at all interested in hearing that the problem will be looked into next week.

Management looks on you as manager of the territory. Indeed, very often they will give you a title such as District Manager, Territorial Manager, and so on. Management looks at it this way: if anything good is going to happen in the territory, you are the one who's going to bring it about. Conversely, when things go wrong in the territory, management holds you responsible.

Work Discipline

Clearly, much work must be done in the territory. It takes considerable personal discipline to get it done because the normal management monitoring controls are often absent in industrial selling. If you work in an office with the boss around, it takes a modest amount of discipline to get to work on time and do your job. Out in the sales territory it's another matter. There is no one to push you out of bed and onto the road in the morning.

There is no one to see if you're calling on the people you should be seeing. Industrial salespeople must manage their own time and this takes self-discipline, which you must have to be successful in selling.

Be on Call

Many organizations expect you to be on call 24 hours a day, 7 days a week. They expect you to respond to emergencies at any time. Such firms expect you to put aside personal factors and private demands to attend to company business when emergencies arise. Such managements feel they have a priority on your time.

Some observers object to such attitudes. Modern individuals often reject these philosophies by maintaining that the company is only buying so many hours a day and that their private time is their own. While there is considerable logic and equity to such beliefs, they do little to solve the basic dilemma of management. Namely, emergencies do not happen for the convenience of one's private life. Emergencies do arise. Customers call in the middle of the night demanding immediate service to some emergency. If the hourly workers go out on strike, someone may have to go and do hard physical work for many hours attending to critical needs. If you say that this isn't what you were hired to do, you may be right. On the other hand, management's attitude is that these things must be done and if you're unwilling to do them, then the company will have to find someone who is willing.

At the time you are considering a job, you should explore carefully what management expects of you. In other words, know beforehand the answer to this question: How much of yourself are you selling?

The basic problem is that in any organization for

which you are employed your work hours are almost totally contingent on the workload placed on you by the market. An extreme example would be in the army. If the enemy attacks at midnight, you don't have much choice; you must work strenuously after hours. A soldier knows no hours. You say, "But I am not a soldier." But recall Betty Harragan's first major point. You are in an army. You are one of the soldiers. The fact is that in many organizations there is a limit to the certainty with which the workload can be anticipated. You must work when there is work that must be done.

Getting promoted

One of the more surprising findings from our Dallas survey of industrial saleswomen was the small percentage of them who had any desire to be promoted into management. The women were happy selling and wanted to stay here. This attitude is not confined to women. We find many salesmen with no desire to advance into management. They realize that management is a totally different endeavor from selling and they like selling. Management is paperwork, offices, conferences, and other related matters with which a true sales personality does not care to be bothered. But let us assume that you have some managerial aspirations. How should you proceed?

Saleswoman—Copying Equipment
I've been in sales for a long time and have also been in management. I was the first female sales instructor with my previous employer and the job was very enjoyable. I've been a branch sales marketing manager where I recruited and trained people. I wanted to change companies, but with the new company I couldn't go into management, I had to start in sales. So at this moment I'm just establishing my sales career so that I'll have a chance to go into management.

Go Where There Are Opportunities to Be Promoted

The key to quick promotion is to work for a rapidly growing firm, one that is going to need many new managers. Promotions come slowly in stagnant concerns where one must wait for normal attrition to make an opening that will allow advancement.

Performance

You do not have to be a top sales producer to be considered for management. Indeed, management is suspicious that the top sales producers will not make good sales managers. The classic case in sales management is the firm that promotes its top sales producer to sales manager only to discover that the factors that made this individual the top producer also make the individual a bad manager. They have lost a good sales representative and gained a lousy manager. When made managers, top salespeople have a strong inclination to be the super salesperson. They spend far too much time still calling on accounts and far too little on the managerial aspects of the job. Wise management looks for things other than sales production as a basis for promoting people.

On the other hand, you're not likely to be considered for promotion unless your sales have been more than satisfactory. You must have a good sales record, even though it need not be considered the top record. It's far more important to prove that you have managerial capabilities than it is for you to be the top salesrep in the organization.

What are these managerial capabilities? Management makes things happen—things we want to happen. It takes some initiative, some know-how, and some vigor. Would you know what to do if you were made manager of a sales force that had been failing to meet the expectations of top management? A good sales manager could walk into the situation with a plan in mind on how to rectify the situation.

Management means knowing how to pick a winning team. You'll not go far in management if you hire the wrong people.

Mangement means developing people and an organization that can get the job done. It means controlling operations to make certain that work is being done as planned. It means having some comprehension of how the whole operation works, how the parts fit together.

Management looks beyond the next customer, the next order, or the next day. Management plans.

Proving Managerial Talents

One plea commonly heard from would-be managers on being told that they have yet to show managerial ability is this: "But how can I prove I have mangerial talent when I haven't been made a manager?" One evening, several months ago I received a call from a Xerox sales representative in southern California. The young man had read my book, *Your Career*, and decided to call to talk over a problem. He had been successful selling copying equipment, but had not been promoted. He said he did not want to spend the rest of his life selling copiers; he wanted to go into management. He had an offer from IBM to sell minicomputers, but he would have to start all over again at the bottom of the ladder and go through the IBM training program to learn all about computer technology, a vastly complex field. I asked him if he had made it known to his boss that he was interested in being promoted. He replied, "Yes, I talked it over at some length with my boss."

"What did he say?" I asked.

"My boss said that when I showed some managerial ability I would be promoted."

I asked if he understood what he had been told. To

the puzzlement I detected, I continued, "Well, now just what did your boss tell you?"

The man stammered and stuttered some more, clearly uncertain of what I was driving at.

So I had to tell him plainly: "You have been working for this man for several years and now he tells you that you will be promoted when you show him some managerial capability. In other words he told you that so far you haven't shown any."

Suddenly, my caller became aware that in his manager's opinion he had done nothing to show managerial talent. This is typical of so many people. They fail to look at their performance through the eyes of management. What does a manager look for in appraising a salesrep's managerial capability?

Paperwork

Paperwork is one of the necessary chores of management. Experience has clearly shown that the person unable to take care of the paperwork necessary to do his or her job is not apt to be successful in management. There is always paperwork that must be done correctly and promptly. The salesrep with managerial talent takes care not only to do all the paperwork on time, but also to do it properly.

Management is serious about the paperwork it wants from salesreps. Consequently, the paperwork you do provides considerable proof that you can handle this portion of whatever managerial tasks might be assigned to you.

Suggestions

The comments, suggestions, and information you send to management regarding your field observations and the ideas you have for improving operations affect management's evaluation of your managerial potential. Do you think like a manager? Do you look at things as a manager looks at them? Or do you go through life always being a worker, displaying a worker's mentality? This is the key question. The person with managerial potential looks at things through the eyes of management and has a managerial prospective on things. Let's take one example. Suppose the company introduces a new product and it's not selling well. The pure salesrep often takes the stance, "I will not waste my time pushing this because I can sell a lot more pushing other products for which less resistance is encountered." The managerial mind sees the situation in this manner: "We all know we'll make more sales spending time on the products for which there is an established demand. It's going to take a lot of time to sell this new product and that is going to hurt our other production. But if the company feels that it's important to get this new product started (there may be some strategic considerations why management wants to pay the price to get into the new market), then I'll get behind it and do my best." What you write in your call reports can sound like a manager evaluating the situation or a salesrep routinely discharging his or her duty. Try to sound like a manager—an intelligent, knowledgeable one!

Recruiting Personnel

One of management's key tasks is the recruiting and selecting of effective sales personnel. It is a difficult art. Management has learned that one of the best sources for obtaining good recruits is from the existing sales force. They often ask the salesreps to stay alert for such people. By all means, be continually aware of this problem. Your managerial stock will soar when top management sees that you are able to spot and attract talented salesreps to the company.

Training

Often, management will place the new sales recruit under an established salesrep for training. How well you execute this training task is important to your managerial future. Training is definitely an important sales management function and good sales trainers are rare.

Company Practices

Some companies won't promote women. They discriminate! While you may choose to work for such a firm and subsequently fight your way up through the courts, this is not the strategy of hardheaded realists. Instead, they suggest that before accepting employment with a company you determine if it is promoting women into management. If it isn't, watch out because this means that you'd be the first so promoted and the life of a pioneer is not an easy one.

Changing Jobs

Sometimes the only way you can get into management is by changing jobs. Often it will become clear to you that you will never be promoted from your present position. If you want management, then you will have to get it elsewhere.

The key to such job mobility is for you to gain as much exposure as possible in your industry and territory. Be active in your trade associations and local sales executives clubs. Let people know who you are and what you can do. And in the proper place, don't be reluctant to let others know that you aspire to management.

Management of personal affairs

Many sales managers refuse to hire people whose personal life is chaotic. A record of marital discord, bankruptcy, or financial troubles may cause automatic rejection. The manager thinks, "How can someone manage a territory when they can't even manage themselves?" Yes, there is a strong bias in business against people who are unable to manage their own lives. Experience indicates that when people are in personal trouble it affects their job performance. Sometimes tangled personal affairs simply take the person off the job too much. In other instances, the mental anguish seriously and adversely affects their performance.

An instance of such personal chaos is this:

Terri was tall, brunette, and vivacious. Physically, she was the epitome of the Texas beauty with her clear skin and blue eyes. She was forceful and appealing, and if she could have foregone the soap opera of her life she could have enjoyed a tremendously successful career in sales. Her soap opera became so consuming it finally became a threat to the time and efforts of my entire staff.

When I first met Terri she was working for a home

builder as a troubleshooter and sales representative. I
met her through a friend and was impressed. I heard
later the builder had fired her and she had left Dallas.
I didn't think too much about it at the time because I
knew the developer and knew he had a reputation for
being harsh. I was surprised a few years later to
receive a phone call from her asking for a job
interview. She told me she had gone to Oklahoma and
had recently moved back to Dallas because she was in
the process of getting a divorce. Terri had a little boy
and wanted desperately to get back into sales. I didn't
have a full-time opening, but I put her on straight
commission. I explained that my company was going
through a restructuring process financially and that if
things went well and if her performance was good we
would work her into a full-time job.

Her performance was brilliant. She landed accounts
that amazed me. She seemed to enjoy working and
seemed to thrive on the public contact. There was just
one problem. She began spending less and less time
working in sales. It soon became apparent that her
life was just one long and painfully drawn-out soap
opera.

The handsome young man she was living with had left
his wife and children in Oklahoma to move in with
her—and she had left her husband for him. They had
fallen in love and braving the disapproval of family
and society had taken up residence together. I'm not a
moralist. What others do with their lives personally is
none of my business. I'm not at all interested unless
in some way what others do reflects on or affects my
life. Terri's emotional state of mind began to play
havoc with my business. Her young man beat her. I

learned of this one day when she came flying into my office several hours late and started weeping hysterically. It appeared Rob (Terri's boyfriend) came home drunk the previous night and beat her. Her face bore the loser's trophies of the fight. I was horrified and sympathetic. I could not believe any man could be so vile and behave in such a manner. I offered a strong shoulder, hours of counseling, and lots of comfort. (I guess the game I have to prevent myself from playing is that of a mother hen. This episode happened years ago and I was not as aware of this trait within my nature as I am now.) The entire office and every employee began hearing daily reports of the tremendous battle being waged between Terri and Rob. Money seemed to be a bit of a problem and she felt trapped by the situation. I was determined to help. Because I was entering a partnership with a different financial structure I was unable to put Terri on a salary—but I did help her develop accounts. I also worked out a trade-out arrangement with an apartment owner to the effect that we would give him advertising in exchange for an apartment. I was thrilled. The apartment was not fancy, but it was not a slum either. It faced a pool, had two bedrooms, and was in a good neighborhood near our office. I knew that Terri's car was paid for and there was a children's nursery nearby. She could, for a time, live very inexpensively until her commissions built up. But best of all, she could escape the terrible emotional and physical conditions in which she was living.

I'll never forget the look Terri gave me when I enthusiastically informed her that I had found her a place to live. It seems that Rob had just bought a very expensive home in an affluent North Dallas area and

Terri was busy decorating it. She declined the apartment. I was stunned. A few nights later I saw Terri and Rob in a nightclub. Apparently, all had been forgiven as they stared dreamily into each others eyes. I began to see what was happening. The soap opera continued. More tears, phone calls, and nervous, worried employees. I discovered one day that Terri had called one of my saleswomen at 2 AM the previous morning in tears. She was calling from a phone booth outside a nightclub. She and Rob were having a fight. Would the saleswoman come and get her? Faithful and dedicated, Diane rushed to the rescue. As she drove up to the club Terri ran across the lot and jumped into Diane's car sobbing hysterically. Suddenly, Rob appeared and he too jumped into her car. Physical blows followed, Terri's earring was ripped from her ear, blood gushed, and Diane was terrified. "Drive," a hysterical Terri would scream. "Stop," an angry Rob would bellow. Diane alternately drove and stopped across the parking lot. It took Diane days to regain her composure and her sales suffered. As for Terri, she soon was her old happy self.

The fights continued with regularity. Apparently, it was a lot of fun to fight and very romantic to make up. My company merely provided the stage and my employees provided the bodies needed to play the supporting roles in the grand drama. I finally terminated Terri. Her soap opera was costing me too much money and time. She went into a rage that she has never gotten over. From some more recent reports I have become a major villain in her opera. She claims that I cheated her financially, overworked her and so on. It does seem she was almost fired recently from her present job. I suspect the soap opera began interfering with her job again. I've also been told that she and Rob are now married and live in a bigger and better home. Terri drives a Mercedes, but she still shows up for work periodically with a broken wrist, black eye, or other such injuries. The soap opera goes on and on. I'm only grateful that my office is no longer the stage for it. Terri's personal affairs were ruining my business.

Self-Development

You've heard it repeatedly: never stop learning. You are never through with your training. While company-training programs are beneficial they are grossly insufficient for fully developing your talents. If you want to develop into a top-flight professional, you will have to be responsible for your own development.

Many people make the mistake of approaching their self-development on a hit-and-miss basis, just reacting to whatever opportunities present themselves at the time. This will not do. There are four areas to consider in devising your development program: reading, educational programs, peer group learning, and post-sale evaluations.

Reading

Top-flight professionals tend to be avid readers of both books and periodicals. Salesreps eagerly read books knowing full well that they're not likely to learn much new from them. As one rep put it, "If I can get just one idea from a book, I'll profit from it hundreds of times over the cost of the book. And even if the book is only a review of what I already know, it's amazing how often I've forgotten the point and can use it. I've been surprised at how I have benefited from reviewing what I already know."

But don't limit your reading to books about selling. Any reading can be beneficial even if it only serves to broaden your conversational abilities and worldly awareness.

More critically, it's important to develop a program of reading periodicals relevant to your business. Every industry has trade journals that cover it and you should be reading them. You should also be reading the trade journals that your customers read. If you sell to women's apparel stores you would want to keep abreast of *Women's Wear Daily*. It's not difficult to find out what magazines your customers read. Just ask them.

Educational Programs

In most metropolitan areas various training is offered to help the salesperson become more proficient. Obviously, not every program will be worth your while. But you will be surprised that even the poorest of programs may at least challenge your thinking and channel it into certain beneficial areas. Many of these programs are inspirational and some salesreps justifiably become bored with the rah-rah, go-get-'em approach offered by them. On the other hand, some people say they benefit from such inspirational messages. They need their battery recharged every now and again.

Peer Group Learning

After your introductory training, you will profit handsomely by learning from your peers, your fellow salespeople. During casual coffee breaks and various social events they will talk shop. And there is the kind soul who likes to be asked for his or her opinion. This person wants to play professor, for doing so makes her feel superior while you are deferring to her experience and expertise. So let her feel superior. You have a lot to learn and if the tuition is the application of a bit of ego balm, pay it. It's cheap! But choose your teachers carefully. You'll not learn much from those who don't know much. Pick the experienced salesrep who knows how to do things and how things work in both the industry and the company.

While many people believe that socializing among salespeople is a waste of time, just an excuse for a bit of imbibing, they are mistaken. Much is learned by everyone from such get-togethers. It's called "communications" by the academic community. While the experts love to extol the virtues of communications, they seldom care to explore just how all these virtuous communications take place. Well, they happen at parties, in the rest rooms, around the water cooler, and the informal chats all around the office. So socialize!

One notable effort to stimulate peer group learning was instituted by a young enterprising sales recruit who talked a small group of colleagues into meeting once a week in the evening for a "Sales Round Table." A specific topic would be chosen each week; then the group would invite some experienced salesrep to talk about that topic.

Post-Sale Evaluations

We have mentioned previously that successful people learn to profit from their experiences. You'll not likely learn much from each experience if you do not consciously stop to ponder what there was to learn from it.

After each sale you should make an appraisal of what went wrong; equally as important, you'll want to appraise what went right during the interview. If you made the sale, try to pinpoint why you got the order. Understand the basis for your success so you can repeat it. Similarly, when you do not get the order, try to figure out why. Often there may have been something in the picture that you were unable to affect. Develop a quick checklist against which to evaluate the attempted sale. Some of the considerations you'll want to include are these:

1. Was the company a good prospect for your goods?
2. Did you do your homework or were you inadequately prepared to handle what you ran into?
3. Were you talking to the real decision maker or were you verbally fencing with some underling who was passing himself off as the boss?
4. Do you understand the prospect's problems?
5. What was the real reason the prospect did not buy?

This list can easily be expanded as needed to meet your particular selling situation, but it should give you some idea of what is involved in a post-sale evaluation. Some sales managers require such evaluations from you after each presentation.

Basic personality traits leading to success

If you were to study the sales management literature on the selection of sales personnel you would be inundated with verbiage on application blanks, personal histories, evaluation of work experience, references, and personal background analysis. Sales managers learn many meaningful things from such background material. Application blanks normally give your track record, which hopefully indicates some of your traits. But what about the person who has yet to establish a record? How does one evaluate people who have had no selling experience? What are the basic factors that lead to success in selling? Let's examine five critical traits that are often overlooked. While these five factors are interrelated, it will be best to discuss them separately for each furnishes a different insight into what it takes to be successful in whatever it is you're trying to do. The five factors are (1) mental toughness, (2) social intelligence, (3) acceptance of responsibility, (4) motivation, and (5) commitment.

Mental Toughness

One individual defined "mental toughness" as "the ability to encounter adversity without allowing it to affect your determination to reach your goal." In other words, you don't quit. More will be said in a later section on motivation about the evils of quitting, but suffice it here to emphasize that people who are mentally tough do not allow past events to deter their determination to get the job done. Mental toughness simply means that when you make up your mind to do something, you do it. You find a way to get the job done.

Mental toughness is tremendously important in selling because most industrial sales representatives often encounter failures. They get it in various ways: "We're satisfied with our present supplier" or "We don't need any today" or "Your prices are too high" or "Get out of here; don't bother me." The litany could go on almost endlessly. You will fail many times for each success. Yet fail you must for success to be born.

Psychologically, some people cannot accept failure. They take rejection personally. One of the biggest causes of failure in selling is that the individual simply cannot stand to be rejected by others. Most of us have a deep-seated desire to be liked by others. We want other people to accept us and take us into their confidence. When you are selling something your relationships with other people are not always that of a close friend, even though you might desire them to be so. If you are hypersensitive to the reactions of other people to you and your product, you are not apt to last long in selling. You cannot allow turndowns, rejections, and obstacles to affect your resolve to get the job done. As some sales experts put it, "The sale starts when the prospect says no." Well, that is an overstatement, but it does reflect the attitude that good salesreps do not allow initial rejection to affect their resolution to make the sale if they are convinced that the prospect needs their proposition and can afford it.

How does one go about measuring mental toughness?

The answer is study the individual's record to see whether he or she carries his assignment through to success or quits. Managers are wary of people who leave every time they face some obstacles. They look for evidence that the individual has licked something. Indeed, I sometimes tell college students that perhaps the biggest reason employers want to hire them is that they have proved that they have sufficient mental toughness to accomplish what they set out to do—graduate from college. They have proved that they were able to discipline themselves to a four-year grind doing many things they found distasteful, doing things not always to their liking.

While the following overlaps with previous discussion, it reiterates how important mental toughness is to most managers.

People often confuse mental toughness with meanness and associate the term with someone who has a nasty disposition. Some of the most outstanding businesswomen I have known were delightful, diplomatic, kind, and feminine. They were also mentally tough. That is, they had the ability to withstand adversity and to make a commitment to complete a project with the utmost excellence possible despite any objections or obstacles that might arise along the way. Mentally tough individuals realize their jobs often entail performing tasks that are not always pleasant. They do not let themselves indulge in the negative emotions of bitterness, anger, and resentment to the extent that they destroy their careers. They know that life is not always fair and are able to cope with failure. They may cry a bit when knocked down, but eventually they will dust off bruised knees and get back on their feet. They learn to look for the lesson to be learned in every failure.

The mentally tough woman—like her male counterpart—learns to live with the fact that not everyone she deals with will like her. She will do her utmost to be tactful and diplomatic at all times, but she will not waste her time worrying about why someone appears not to like her or seems to be working against her. While she will not be afraid of making the extra effort of going the extra mile, she will have the strength to walk away from a situation when she realizes it is hopeless.

Part of being mentally tough means never making excuses for yourself and always accepting responsibilities. Emotional problems never take precedence over your work. If you fight with a husband or lover, if you have a conflict with a teenage offspring, or if you are going through some traumatic emotional experience it can be very tempting to carry these problems to work or even not to show up for work at all. This is when you begin playing the game I referred to earlier as soap opera. Remember Terri.

Soap opera can be one of the most wasteful and insidious games of all. It's a game that moves from stage to stage with the same actresses repeating the same tired lines—only the setting and the supporting players change. It's a game that is not only time consuming and emotionally exhausting, it can prove to be the total destruction of a career. We all have times and periods of upheaval during our lives. It is important that when we are faced with an emotional trauma we pull ourselves together, force ourselves into the office, and put our entire effort and concentration into our project. During the periods in my life when I have done this while faced with emotional traumas I was later amazed to discover working actually helped me cope with those problems.

The problems resolved themselves over a period of time while I was doggedly building a career. There are women, however, who become totally enmeshed in their emotional problems and I suspect their soap opera existence becomes a way of life and entertainment for them.

Mental Toughness versus Fear

The mentally tough individual is not immune to self-doubt and human weakness. Like others, the mentally tough person will have to battle and conquer a formidable enemy—the fear of failure.

It's difficult to understand how so many people despite numerous gifts and talents can be defeated at times by a fear of failure. Fear of failure can be so overwhelming that some people never attempt anything of any importance. They will not take the chance to succeed. To accomplish anything worthwhile in life involves taking a chance, and part of taking a chance includes risking failure.

I had a very interesting phone call one day from a lady I would later meet socially. This woman informed me that she received tremendous enjoyment from reading my column because of my references to many personal experiences. She went on to say she kept a very tight circle drawn around herself in life allowing very little opportunity for different experiences. The reason for this, she explained, was that she wanted to do everything perfectly in life and thereby attempted little. Thus she felt she would run a much smaller risk for failure. Dumbfounded, I had no response to this comment. Further, I felt that since I did not know her, it was not my place to tell her how to conduct her life. While talking to her, though, I could not help picturing her as a very little and cautious old lady. Imagine my surprise when I was introduced to her several weeks later and found her vivacious, young, and charming. She has so much to offer, but has decided that failure is the very worst thing that can happen to her in life; therefore, to avoid failure she has set limits regarding what she will try to do.

Why do we have such an enormous fear of failure? Perhaps it stems from a background where many of us were expected to live up to what seemed a perfect ideal—one that seemed flawless. Perhaps it stems from critical parents who warned us repeatedly not to fail and actually destroyed our initiative. It may be because of our religious background, which for many is fundamental and places great emphasis on sin and hell—the ultimate failure and final punishment.

Many outstanding people, and some of our greatest achievers, have experienced their greatest growth during periods of failure. The greatest lesson we have to learn from failure is that we survive it. It takes maturity to finally realize we will not be the first or the last to fail in an endeavor. It comes as a great shock when we discover that we're not unique in our inabilities and that other people often aren't interested in them. We finally realize this and simply lift ourselves up and begin anew.

I once had an interesting discussion with a young man who was my editor. An excellent writer, he was compassionate and demonstrated a warm personality that made everyone love him. He was with me during some hard times. No one could have worked harder or been more loyal. I noticed, however, that when things got too rough that he would go on wild drunken binges. One day we were discussing this in my office and he confessed that he had an overwhelming fear of failure and was terribly concerned that our business would fail.

I listened carefully and said, "Tell me, just what is the worst thing that can happen if we do fail?"

He was silent for a while and answered, "Well, not much, I guess."

"We would simply pick ourselves up and start over," I said. "The only thing is we wouldn't make the same mistakes the second time around."

When he left he acted as if a great burden had been lifted from his shoulders. I was glad. I had fought that same battle with a fear of failure during many long, sleepless nights.

When I first began a career in sales I would figuratively bleed when someone turned me down for the order. I was so afraid of rejection that I would drag my sales manager along while I made the presentation. She became my security blanket. If I was refused, I would almost burst into tears. I suspect now that some of my poor advertisers suffered also when they saw the look on my face when they told me no. Salespeople need to understand that a rejection is no more to be taken personally than it is to be taken permanently. In later years it was not unusual for me to call on someone for as long as four years without getting an order.

One of my first employees impressed me profoundly with her mental toughness. In many ways she had much working against her, but because she had such mental toughness she enjoyed outstanding success.

I never understood why I hired Diane. A woman I knew who worked as a secretary had told me about her and described her much differently from what I later would describe her myself. I mentioned that I was looking for someone to train in sales and asked the secretary to send her friend in.

That same day I looked up from my desk to see a pitiful looking waif staring fixedly at the floor. Her blonde hair hung in long curls, she was wearing a blue rain coat, she was about 5'2", and seemed to be about 17. After she mumblingly introduced herself, I began questioning her, knowing full well that she would never make it in sales and that I would never hire her. She was 23, a college graduate, had tried teaching and hated it, and desperately needed a job. She was running out of money and was too proud to tell her parents. She did not want to go home. She wanted to make it on her own. I hired her; I'll never know why. I was convinced I had made a mistake the moment she left.

To get things over with as painlessly as possible, since I was convinced that I had made a mistake, I gave her some information briefly and literally threw her to the wolves. I was busy and I didn't expect her to make it.

In looking back I realize how unfair I was to this young woman while I tried so hard with others who failed. I began to see a glimmer of the jewel that she was when she showed up in my office later with a glint in her eye and a determined thrust to her jaw. "Well, what happened," I asked.

"They threw me out," she answered.

"And . . . ," I asked.

"I went back in and they took an ad," was her determined reply.

I then began training her in earnest and she proved to be one of the most valuable employees that I have ever had.

Let me explain my lack of consideration for this young woman. It was in the early 1970s. Most of our advertising was from builders and we were in a *recession. I was scared stiff. Builder after builder was declaring bankruptcy and the survivors were either cutting back their advertising drastically or completely eliminating their advertising budget. I didn't know if I could make it. Diane proved to be a godsend. Like a sponge, she absorbed everything I taught her. Together, she and I filled the paper consistently with $50 ads. I've never known anyone to work as hard as she did. It was ironic because she didn't seem to like people and once told me bluntly that she didn't particularly like me. I informed her that it didn't bother me a bit. As long as she would take direction from me and apply it, I could tolerate her dislike. She worked for me for four years. Her husband is an outstanding artist and she now works for him. She was a tremendous achiever and I think of her fondly. Occasionally, one of her old customers will ask about her and it's not uncommon for them to say, "You know, I wasn't too fond of that little girl when she began calling on me, but she was so determined she finally won my respect and I really think a lot of her."*

Why did she do so well? She had no experience. She gave the impression of being a guarded and suspicious person. She was unsure of herself, but did have one ingredient—mental toughness—and that was enough.

Social Intelligence

Most psychologists prefer to begin the study of personality with an analysis of intelligence, for it seems to form the basic foundation for the human experience. For many years psychologists felt that they really had a good handle on measuring intelligence and knew what it was. However, they have grown wiser and come to realize that even intelligence is a difficult behavioral characteristic to pin down. Where they once thought they could measure abstract intelligence rather accurately with their so called I.Q. tests, now they're not quite certain what they are measuring with their I.Q. examinations.

There are several types of intelligence. First, there is abstract intelligence, which is the ability to perceive and comprehend abstract thoughts. The person well endowed with abstract intelligence quickly grasps the meanings of symbols and the relationships between things in the environment. They can handle the symbols we call numbers and words with great skill—mathematics and vocabulary. They do well on I.Q. tests because such instruments are heavily loaded with mathematics and English skills. Certainly abstract intelligence is important. But not nearly as important to success in selling as social intelligence.

In many careers, particularly selling, we've come to realize that social intelligence is far more important to success than abstract intelligence. Social intelligence is one's ability to perceive the proper thing to say and do in a social situation. They know how to deal with other people. There are some people who have the knack of making other people like them. They do and say the right things. These people do well in selling. While social skills can be a great help in selling, do not conclude that without them all is lost. There are many people who compensate for a lack of social grace by hard work and ingenuity.

Acceptance of Responsibility

In education we have long been concerned about those people possessed of adequate intelligence who nevertheless flunk out of school. They were unable to get the job done although possessing the tools with which to do it. We call them underachievers. The underachiever's counterpart is the overachiever—the person able to accomplish far more than one would have the right to expect based on the tools with which the person has to work. Unfortunately, there are far more underachievers in the world than overachievers. Some years ago the psychologists at the University of Oklahoma made an intensive study of this phenomenon by analyzing the personality characteristics of the overachiever in contrast to those who failed to do what was expected of them. The results were surprisingly clearcut. When they asked overachievers why they came to college, such answers were heard as "I wanted to" or "I want to be such and such and needed a college degree to do it." Clearly, they came to college because of a decision they made. When you asked them why they had difficulty in a certain course you would hear such explanations as "I just didn't like the subject matter and didn't work at it" or "I didn't study" or "I was playing around." They took responsibility for the failure. When they were successful in a class, you'd hear answers of this sort: "I really liked the teacher" or "I liked that subject"—all normal answers. But talk to the underachievers and a striking difference is noted immediately. When asked why they came to college, the underachievers' responses would be: "My parents wanted me to come" or "It's the thing to do" or "All my friends are here." They came to college because others wanted them to come. They didn't make the decision; someone else made it for them. When asked why they had failed a course, such explanations were given as "The teacher had it in for me" or "My high school didn't prepare me properly for that" or "No one has ever taught me how to study." Every failure was blamed on someone else. The underachievers accepted no responsibility for their failures.

Thus one key to your success depends on your acceptance of the responsibility for your successes and failures. You must realize that if you succeed you will only do so because of your own efforts. True, other people can help you succeed. You can learn from others, but it is you who makes the choice of whom to listen to and from whom you'll accept guidance. And if you fail, it will be because of your own shortcomings. Don't try to blame it on anyone else, because you're the one who managed to get yourself into the position.

The importance to the manager of this willingness to accept responsibility is that people who refuse to accept responsibility for their actions are essentially unmanageable. How can a manager possibly have a meaningful discussion with a salesrep about a poor sales performance if that person blames the poor performance "on competitive conditions," "poor products," and so on. As long as the person is alibiing for his or her failure, little learning will take place. Why should individuals change their behavior if they don't think their previous behavior was responsible for the failure? They won't. Until an individual mentally admits responsibility for a failure, he or she will not profit from that failure. The overachiever stands back and examines failure to see what can be learned from it. You should improve yourself each time you fail. You must ask yourself, "Now what went wrong here and how can I keep from making the same mistake again?" This is the key to self-development.

The sales manager discovers a person's acceptance of responsibility by probing into the person's failures. Everyone has failures and blemishes on his or her record. Locate some failure and ask the individual to explain it. When you hear a string of alibis, know that you're talking with an underachiever.

The basic proposition in industrial selling is that the company gives you the responsibility for selling its products or services in a territory and from that point what happens is up to you. If you do not realize and take full responsibility for your territory, you will be headed for some difficult times in selling.

Commitment

We have talked about the virtues of mental toughness at great length; but taken alone, mental toughness may not yield the positive results you seek. It must be directed toward whatever goals you strive to reach. And this requires commitment by you to achieve your goals, to get what you want.

Now all this sounds absurdly simple. Unfortunately, experience indicates that it is not. A young woman of great talent and unlimited potential was absolutely certain when she was in college that she wanted to manage her own business. She knew that the corporate world was not for her. Anyone talking with her would have taken an oath that she and her own enterprise would soon find each other because she seemed to want it so badly and had the necessary talent. But she wasn't sufficiently committed to her dream for it to become a reality. A young man swayed her toward other goals. A marriage and two jobs later she had given up all hopes of her own business. She had not been committed to her stated goals. They were only her wishful thinking.

And this is exactly what most people's goals are—wishful thinking. They say, "Gee, I sure would like to do such and such. It would be nice. I hope it happens." Well, it won't likely happen if you don't make it happen, and this requires a firm commitment from you.

A "commitment" of the type we speak of here is a contract that you make with yourself. You mentally agree with yourself to accomplish something and then feel duty bound to honor that contract. If you can't perform— can't deliver the goods—on contracts you make with yourself, just what contracts in life will you honor? Must you be hauled into court to be made to do what you promised yourself you would do? But the only court with jurisdiction over your personal vows to yourself are in your own mind and you are the judge and jury. Most people are far too lenient in their own self-judgments.

If you now have concluded that this matter of setting goals and making commitments to achieving them is a serious matter worthy of considerable soul-searching, then you have gotten the message. You are ready to think about how to find the motivation for fulfilling your commitments.

Motivation

The locker room walls at the University of Oklahoma during the Bud Wilkinson years come vividly to mind each time the subject of motivation arises. Over the door that opened onto the turf of Owens Stadium was a large red and white sign that urged, "Play like a champion today." Other signs were appropriately placed that proclaimed the usual cliches found in most athletic locker rooms, "When the going gets tough, the tough get going," and "Quitters never win, winners never quit." At the University of Kansas the famed basketball coach, the late Dr. Forrest C. Allen, reminded his players time and again that to be a champion one must want to be one so very badly that anything else is unacceptable. Coach Allen believed that the difference between champions and the also-rans was largely motivation. He primarily concerned himself with motivating his players, not so much during games as throughout life. At all times he urged them to work hard to improve their skills. It's too late on game day to do much about your talent. Success is the culmination of a long series of daily efforts that are often painful, boring, and even difficult. Short cuts are seldom found.

Bud Wilkinson continually preached to his lads that the very same lessons they learned on the football field would carry them to success in whatever endeavor they chose to undertake in the future. Coach Wilkinson was a consumate motivator. One story may provide insights into how highly he values the mental side of human endeavors. His 1956 national championship Oklahoma football team was trailing Maryland 6–0 at halftime in the Orange Bowl. The national championship was on the line. The Maryland team was not only very big and tough, but was most adept at its trade. They had learned their lessons well. At halftime, the Oklahoma team retreated to the locker room to regroup and to learn what Coach Wilkinson proposed they do to meet this unexpectedly vigorous Maryland team. Coach Wilkinson was silent as the trainers ministered to the players aches and pains and sutured their wounds. Shortly before it was time to return to the field, Coach Wilkinson gathered the squad around him and quietly related this tale. "There was an old wise man in a small town who was highly esteemed by all in the village. A young aspirant to the wise man's esteemed position plotted to disgrace him. He confided his plot to a friend. During the town meeting at which the wise man would preside, the young man would hold a canary in his hand. He would then ask the wise man what he held. The wise one would reply 'a bird.' The young pretender would contemptuously say, 'Of course, any fool can see that, but is it dead or alive?' If the wise one replied 'alive,' the young man would ever so gently crush the canary, then open his hand to expose the dead bird. If on the other hand, the wise man replied 'dead,' the young man would release the canary to fly away, thus embarrassing the old man. The eventful day arrived and the young man confronted the wise one with the dilemma: 'Is the bird dead or alive?' The wise man looked at the youngster and replied solemnly, 'As you will my son, as you will.'"

Coach Wilkinson looked around at the silent room, paused most potently, and said, "Gentlemen, as you will, as you will" and left the room. The final score was 21–6, Oklahoma. The team had been taught quite well that if they wanted something bad enough they could have it—a point we've made throughout this book. Achieving what you want is solely a matter of willpower and motivation.

While this material on athletic endeavors may seem irrelevant to many readers, particularly those without athletic backgrounds, experience indicates otherwise.

Successful people know about the importance of motivation. Truly, motivation is the key to success to any endeavor that you choose to undertake. Everyday, all over the world, in every city and town, people are starting to work in new jobs. A few of them will ultimately realize great success. Most will not. Yet each begins wishing that someday he or she will enjoy the success so desperately sought. What is it that causes some people to scale undreamed heights, while others fall into mediocrity at best or failure and despair at worst? Motivation is not easy to understand because of its innumerable dimensions, only some of which are known to us.

In examining motivation, we will approach it several ways. At times it will seem that we will be using different words for just about the same concepts. And perhaps we are. But we do so to give you a clearer picture of the subject. Where one approach might not be particularly clear, another might. But first let's define some of the key terms that will be used. Let's examine the much used and misused word, "success." What is it? Many critics of our culture claim that we are too preoccupied with achieving success and that we unduly put down people we consider unsuccessful. True, but nevertheless such is the reality of the world in which we live. The successful are esteemed and the unsuccessful shunned. That is the way it is and there is little you or I can do to change the world regardless of our desire to do so. The old cliches "Success begats success" or "Nothing succeeds like success" are certainly true. For some reason all sorts of good things seem to happen to people who others consider successful.

What is success?

It is impossible to define success in concrete terms. Certainly, money is one important yardstick by which people measure success. It is difficult to do much without money. And the more money you have, the more successful other people think you are. These points are so obvious that little is to be gained by belaboring them. But we should point out that many people have all the money they want, but still consider themselves unsuccessful. Conversely, there are people others think are impoverished financially, but who consider themselves successful. Success is not solely a matter of money.

A case can be made that you are successful if you truly believe that you are. Similarly, you are unsuccessful if you believe that you are. But the question arises: what causes you to believe that you are a success or a failure? Here the self-concept theory is helpful. It is an all-encompassing theory of motivation. It tells why we do what we do. It begins with four self-concepts, the *real self*, the *ideal self*, the *real other self*, and the *ideal other self*.

Your "real self" is what you really think of yourself at the present time. It is an all-encompassing set of thoughts about who you are and what you can do. Many people have well-defined *real-self* concepts. Others, particularly young people, have yet to develop clear-cut *real-selves* because they haven't had the experiences needed to know who they are and what they can do. As a general principle, the older you become, the more well defined your self-concepts become.

Your *"ideal-self"* concept is how you would like to see yourself. It is what you would like to believe about yourself, your skills, and your nature. These are your personal goals. Both of these self-concepts are quite personal to you.

Your public image is another matter. Your *"real other self"* concept is what you think other people think of you—how they view you. Your *"ideal other* self" is how you would like other people to see you. It is what you want other people to think of you. The key element to understand is that the individual's every action not only must be compatible with these self-concepts, but also in some way must move one or both of the real selves toward the respective ideal selves. Moreover, people generally refuse to do things that are incompatible with their self-concepts or that may jeopardize them.

While this entire book could be devoted to exploring the significance of the self-concept theory to motivation, the important point here is this: your ideal self-concepts determine your motivation. Where you set your goals determines where you go. As someone once said, "Don't be afraid to reach for the stars. You may not get any, but you won't come up with a handful of mud either." You must realize that these ideal self-concepts—your goals— are not chiseled in stone. They will change with your experiences. And you can change them as you will, hopefully for the better. Indeed, one of the most heartwarming experiences a teacher enjoys is watching a student's self-concepts improve as he or she discovers new capabilities previously thought beyond his or her reach. One young man had wandered aimlessly through high school with a most undistinguished record. He was mostly noted for his athletic talents. Certainly, no one thought him a scholar. He certainly entertained no special self-concepts about his intellect or academic promise. For a variety of reasons irrelevant to this discussion, his teachers had managed to convey to him that he was somewhat less than worthy. Upon receiving a letter from the President of the United States which opened with the salutation, "Greetings," the young man found himself in the employ of the United States Navy where for the first time he was evaluated by people who knew nothing of him. All that counted on his test scores were the answers that he gave. The tests were graded impartially by people who knew only his serial number. The chief petty officer walked into the barracks one day and asked: "Where is Seaman Jones?" The young man immediately hit the deck and identified himself. The CPO smiled (a rare occurrence for him) and said, "Congratulations, word just came from Washington that you scored the highest ever on the test" (an electronic service school final test). The young man was shocked. Additional counseling in the navy disclosed that he had an exceedingly high IQ. He tested amazingly high in all aspects. The young man was deeply affected. In all his previous experiences the teachers had either failed to perceive his abilities or had carefully kept them from him. The young man's athletic career suddenly became secondary. After his discharge from the navy he went to college and achieved a PhD in physics. He now leads a distinguished career in his profession. The point of the story is that once this man's self-concept changed through an experience, his goals were altered. He set his sights higher and he achieved more. Prior to this time, he was completely unaware that it was possible for him to achieve such accomplishments.

And this is the point of this chapter. Most young people today do not believe they have what it takes to reach the top, whatever that top might be. Believing it is impossible to climb to high places, they do not make the efforts to discover the steps that lead to great heights. Their behavior remains that of the average person mired down in mediocrity.

Do not conclude based on the last actual example that you must be a genius to succeed. It would be all too easy for you to fail to identify with the previous story by dismissing it with the thought, "Well, that fellow was exceptional; I'm not." If you allow these thoughts to come into your mind, then you are making a very serious mistake.

All experience clearly shows that the vast majority of people have more than adequate skills and abilities to be successful at almost anything they care to undertake. We use only a fraction of our abilities and work at a small portion of our capacity. There are many people of below-average mentality who are extremely successful in business because they have learned to use what little God gave them most effectively. This is the key to success: learning to use effectively what you've got. Be assured that you have a great deal more going for you than you think. You can accomplish much if you will only give yourself a chance to do so. Later, we will discuss what it will take for you to have such a chance.

Now, however, let's talk about the people who will climb to success. They are few in number, but they do believe they will succeed. Right from the start they know they are winners. A professor of business administration related in a book about driving into a large town one night with a young college student who was, in a few years, to become one of the nation's leading professional golfers, a two-time U.S. Open champion—Hale Irwin. There were people in the golfer's hometown who did not believe he had what it took to be successful on tour.

After all, many eager young golfers can hit the ball out of sight and tear up the local links. But succeeding on the pro-tour is another matter. It takes a lot more than an ability to hit the ball. Yet that night, driving in with this young man, the professor knew beyond any doubt that this youngster was to enjoy great success. There wasn't a doubt in the golfer's mind that he was going to be tremendously successful. He knew exactly what he wanted and what it was going to take to get it and was willing to pay the price. This young man had started his climb toward the top when he was 14 years old and never doubted that he would be successful.

At the time of this writing, in a similar situation, the professor has a young woman in training to become a leader in the fashion world. One only needs to hear her talk to know that she is going to be a tremendous success. She has set her goals and wants to achieve them badly enough so that she is paying the price to learn and develop her skills. The important factors to appreciate here are that these people truly believe, even know, down deep that they are going to succeed. They approach their work with the I'm-going-to-the-top attitude. Believing that they will succeed and knowing that it can be done, these people study and observe the behavior of other successful people, thereby learning their patterns of success and the routes they take to achieve their goals. Belief in success is the one absolutely essential ingredient for success. Belief in success is behind every successful business, church, and political organization. It is the power—the driving force— behind great books, plays, scientific discoveries, and business success.

Disbelief is a negative power. When you have in your mind disbeliefs or doubts, reasons to support such are attracted and there is never any shortage of reasons why failure is imminent. The president of a large corporation once confided why he had undertaken a rather bold controversial venture. He said, "Everybody on my board and my staff was against it. They offered hundreds of reasons why we shouldn't do it. But I countered them all by saying there was one reason why we were going to do it and that was because it had to be done. And by God, it will be done." And it was!

Disbelief is rampant. It's a drug on the market. Doubters are to be found on every corner. Think a minute and you will understand why most people want to be doubters, why they want to disbelieve. It is easy to fail. The easiest thing in the world to do is to lose. It takes no talent to go into business and fail or to go out on the athletic field and lose. Anyone can do that. It takes a great amount of effort and dedication to be a winner. Many people simply do not want to make the effort to be a winner; they are just plain lazy. Thus they can hide behind doubts and disbelief to justify their lack of dedication to the task at hand. These people's disbelief is a rationalization for their failure to put forth an effort. The lazy student rationalizes, "Why should I work hard when I haven't got a chance anyway?"

A psychology professor at a leading university related this incident. The university at which he was teaching had a long history of winning on the football field. The university's teams were highly respected for many years, but had fallen on hard times and had not had a winning season for more than a decade. An excellent new coach had been hired and although the team was stocked with considerable talent, it continued to lose. The coach was frustrated. The psychologist and coach had become good friends. In his desperation, the coach asked for help. "Joe, I'm at the end of my rope. I'm about to resign. We have the talent out there; I know it.

These kids are great, but they seem to be losers. They don't seem to realize that they can be winners. Take last Saturday. We had State down 21–0 late in the third quarter and those kids stood around trying to find a way to lose, which they finally managed to do. There wasn't a reason in the world for us to lose to that team; yet we did. They don't know what winning is all about. Can you do something about it?"

The psychology professor undertook what he considered to be one of the most significant projects of his life—instilling into individuals the idea that they can win if they want to win.

One management writer has been associated in various relationships with several great national championship teams and unfortunately has also been associated with some losing efforts. He said, "It's difficult to describe the differences in the noises you hear from the winners and those heard from the losers. Winners make totally different sounds. They talk in different terms. They say different words. They think different thoughts. They are different people. Thoughts of losing seldom cross their mind. They have complete confidence that they will win. But losers don't believe they can win. They play to minimize their pain."

Thus it is not happenstance that people who evaluate others place great reliance on the sounds that they hear. Winners talk like winners while losers talk differently. Now that the subject of winning and losing has been introduced, let's talk about it.

How
to win

While we will discuss many factors that are important to developing a winning attitude, never forget that
the essence of winning is to want whatever it is you
want so badly that you are willing to pay the price
necessary to get it. You don't make it to the top *without*
paying a price. The price may be long hours, less time
with your family, much travel, and so on. Success has its
price and you'll not be willing to pay it unless you're
sufficiently motivated to do so.

Look Like a Winner

Most winners look like winners. They dress well.
They look good. They carry themselves proudly because
they are proud. They're proud of who they are, what
they are, what they have done, and what they can do.
Conversely, many people disclose they are losers by
their appearance and demeanor. The fact is that most
people have little else to judge you by than your appearance, the car you drive, or where you live. From
such evidence, they conclude whether you are a winner
or a loser. Argue as you might with the injustice of such
an evaluation system, the fact is that this is how the real
world works and there is little you can do about it. If
you want the opportunity to show your real talent, don't
hide it behind the facade of a loser. Of course, winning
is not merely a matter of the props one uses. Plenty of

losers look good. People are continually fooled by appearances. But note, one person will begin a relationship with another believing that the other person is a winner until the evidence proves otherwise. People who look like losers are seldom mistaken for anything else.

Associate with Winners

It has often been said that you are judged by the company you keep. And this is true. If you associate with people known to be losers, others will likely think the same of you. If you associate with successful people, not only will you likely be judged to be successful, but also you will learn a lot about what it takes to be successful. The only thing you will learn from losers is how to lose. If you want to learn how to win, then you will have to learn those lessons from winners for the losers don't know them.

If You Can't Win, Don't Play

You're not apt to develop the image of being a winner if you continually lose at what you do. John was a young man of many talents, but poker and golf were not among them. He was a big loser at the poker table and on the golf links. Yet he continually insisted on playing. He not only paid a financial price for his folly, he developed among the people who knew him the image of being a loser. They all laughed at John and considered him a fool. John hadn't learned the lesson that if he was going to play poker and golf he had best learn how to play those games or not play them at all. No one would have thought anything about it had John stayed out of the poker game and had not played golf.

The relationship ended in tragedy for he developed such a loser's complex that it ruined his family life. He quit his job and moved from the area. John had yet to learn that one should not play games at which one is not adept. If you can't win, don't play. It certainly does not sound like a sporting attitude but we are not discussing sports. We are concerned with your career, your success, your life. And that is not a sporting matter.

In fact, few things hurt your image as badly as being a constant loser. The best way to stop losing is don't lose—don't play. But if you must play, learn to play to win.

At the time of this writing one of the authors is secretly teaching a comrade how to play golf. The colleague is quite provoked at two of his "friends" who are snubbing him; they play in the mid 80's while he scores around 100. Since he is such a bad golfer in their eyes, they are not inviting him to play with them. He opened the venture with the plea, "Teach me how to play golf in the low 80's. I want to beat their brains out one of these days. I don't care how long it takes or what I've got to do, but I'm going to take them out and nail them to the barn door." He's going to learn to win before he plays their game. He's making nice progress. Motivation is certainly not one of the elements lacking in the picture. He will get the job done because the motivation is there to do it.

As we go to press my colleague just informed me that he won a golf tournament at the Southwest Conference meeting of faculty representatives with scores of 82 and 86. He was determined to be a winner.

Success Is Learned

Many people are successful largely because they learned to be successful as children. They observed successful roles and emulated them. The point was driven home vividly during one of the author's academic programs in which a simulation (game) was undertaken in which any student who wanted to be the president of a company could be so simply by volunteering. From a class of 200 college seniors, only 7 wanted to be president. As the semester passed, the author came to know these 7 presidents rather well. An interesting fact emerged. The father of each of the volunteer presidents was a president of a substantial corporation. The students had learned how to be president from an early age and were not afraid of the responsibility. To them, being president was just as normal and natural as breathing. To the other students in the class, being president—being successful—was a frightening thought. They didn't know what a president did. It looked like work. They might fail at the job. So they decided not to play president. The same observation was made in subsequent classes.

Many people are successful simply because they learned how to be successful at home at an early age. They are in a position to observe success in action. They see how their mother or father put together deals and make money. Truly, individuals who lack such patterns to copy are at a disadvantage, but not an insurmountable one. Many people without suitable parental roles to copy have selected other people to copy upon realization that they had little to learn from their parents.

The important fact to realize is that success is learned. It can be learned and you can learn it. All you've got to do is find out how to learn it. And you will not learn how to be successful if you are not motivated to do so. Thus we're back to our starting point, observing that the keystone to success is motivation. You can't change the amount of ability that you are born with, but you can certainly change the way you use your ability if you are sufficiently motivated to do so.

Cop-outs

As we have seen fear is the number one enemy of success. Many people fail to seek success because they fear failure. Take the young lad in high school who is afraid to ask the young lady of his dreams for a date for fear that she will say no, will reject him. Egos can be so delicate that people will refuse to seek victory just to avoid rejection or failure. It is more important to them to not fail than to win. Many people don't go into business for themselves because they are afraid they might fail. Students avoid difficult classes that might be of great help because they are afraid of failure. The successful personality doesn't worry about failure. J.C. Penney failed in his first business, but that didn't stop him. He simply picked himself up and started again. Most successful people have failed at some time or another in their lives. Many of them have failed many times. But what difference does it make how many times you fail if in the end you achieve what you want? If you reach your goals, failure is beside the point. The proper way to look at failure is to see it as a learning experience. We learn through our mistakes or at least we should. Granted, many people don't, but through failure success can be born. One top corporate executive made the statement that he prefers to hire people who have been through a business bankruptcy. He was quoted in *Forbes* magazine as saying, "You learn many lessons in bankruptcy that can only be learned by going through that experience." Whether a person fails or not is not nearly as important as what happens after the failure. Do you quit or go on?

One of the advantages the athlete has over people who have no athletic experience is that failure is the rule. The golfer knows that every shot is, in some degree, a mistake. Perfection is not to be expected. One must learn to live with those failures, yet, in the end prevail. The classic case on the golf course is the poor soul who lets his failures get the best of him mentally, thus ruining the entire game. The professional golfer knows that the only thing that really matters is the immediate shot to be made. All preceding shots are history and nothing can be done about them. Also nothing can be done about future shots until it is time to make them. The only thing that's important is the stroke to be made at the moment. The football player learns that every play is a conglomeration of mistakes. The opposing players are seldom where they are suppose to be. Coaches like to draw Xs and Os on the blackboard but the experienced football players know that plays don't work as they are drawn. The linebacker is not standing around waiting for you to take him out of the play and when you get there to throw your block the other guy knocks you down. The backs know that the holes are not always where they are suppose to be. Linemen miss their blocks, but so what. Somehow we forge victory from all failures.

One of the healthiest attitudes you can develop is to be able to fail and look another person right in the eye, admit you failed, and know both the reason why that failure occurred and what you're going to do to avoid the same mistake in the future. You will never learn from your failures until you admit them and take full responsibility for them. Many people try to project their failures onto failings of others. The reason they fail is because somebody else did something wrong, not because of anything they did. People with such attitudes seldom learn much from their failure.

The Taste of Winning

Sally Moore is a woman in her middle thirties with three children. She is presently selling real estate with tremendous success in Dallas. This young woman's success is accelerating as her motivation increases with the sweet taste of money. For the first time she is making a large sum of money that is all her own. She can see it, feel it, count it, and spend it as she likes. And her financial success is making her life a lot more enjoyable. She said, "You know, all my life I've put down money and the people who had it. That was because I didn't have any and never knew what it was like to have money. I didn't know what money would buy. Now that I'm making some money, I know what I was missing and I don't intend to miss any more of it."

Hustle

Sales managers are particularly fond of the "hustling" salesrep. But what is hustle?

Successful saleswoman Sally Moore writes of hustle like this:

What Is Hustle?

Hustle is doing something that everyone
is absolutely certain can't be done.
Hustle is getting the sale because you got there first
or stayed with it after everyone else gave up.
Hustle is shoe leather and elbow grease and sweat and
missing lunch.
Hustle is getting prospects to say "yes" after they've
said "no" twenty times.
Hustle is doing more for a customer than the other
guy is doing for him.
Hustle is believing in yourself and the business
you're in.
Hustle is the sheer joy of winning.
Hustle is being the sorest loser in town.
Hustle is hating to take a vacation because you might
miss a piece of the action.

Hustle is heaven if you're a hustler.
Hustle is hell if you're not.

Many people are not motivated to be successful because they have never tasted the fruits of success. They don't know what success will buy. What you've never experienced, you'll not likely understand. Thus one of the big barriers to motivation is a lack of understanding of what is to be gained by working hard. People are fond of saying that money can't buy happiness, but poverty doesn't buy much either.

Winning: A Matter of Percentages or Skill?

I often hear people state confidently that selling is a game of percentages. The more you play, the more you win; or the more people you call on, the more you sell.

There is an element of truth to this philosophy, but if you think this is the sole means of success, you can have some ego-deflating experiences and some dismal failures.

Selling is an art that requires skill and technique, along with patience, character, and creativity. People who are top professionals in sales are constantly enrolling in self-help courses. They realize that a good sales individual can never know too much. If people find themselves in the position of no longer having anything left to learn about their service or product or the selling of it, they have reached the point when they should move on to more challenging work.

Gone are the days when a peddler could drive down the back roads to rural America assured that when he displayed his wares to the lonely, overworked wives he would make a profit with very little effort. Today, people are bombarded by so many inducements that they are confused and wary about why and what they should buy. The saleswoman who doesn't believe in what she is selling, but who deliberately uses pressure techniques to obtain an order is not a salesperson; she's a con artist. Unfortunately, it is this type of individual, as we've previously mentioned, who long ago created the negative image that shadows the endeavors of the honest, hard-working individual in sales.

I personally cannot sell anything that I do not avidly believe in. I learned this painfully many years ago when I allowed myself to be lured away from a major paper by a man who owned a series of suburban shoppers. It took him six months to convince me to join him. As I became increasingly disillusioned with the new management that had taken over the newspaper for which I worked, and the dead-end place that I had reached in my career, his offers were repeated and seemed increasingly attractive.

Not only did he offer me much more money than I was currently making, but I began to rationalize that since his company was small I would have a real creative outlet and a new challenge. I felt that I was functioning as a very small and insignificant cog in a very huge and impersonal machine. I felt that not only were my accomplishments never to be recognized, but also that they really didn't matter very much to management. These feelings resulted in my quitting my job and joining the **Suburban Seducer.** *In the following months I learned a valuable lesson, which I can sum up here as "Woman does not live by bread alone."*

At first everything was fine. The pay was excellent and I was accorded the respect of a veteran professional who had made the big time on a major newspaper. It was flattering and ego building to say the least. I brought in several new accounts and enthusiastically began creating promotional ideas that I felt might increase the appeal of the paper. I felt that at last I was realizing financial security.

Then some discouraging factors began appearing. My advertisers, many of them good friends, reported to me candidly that they were not realizing any results from the dollars they invested. These reports were being made consistently. I noticed a high turnover in personnel. I rarely saw the same person at a desk for more than four weeks and I began to hear rumors. The distribution manager, whose confidence I had gained, confirmed my worst fear. Although the number of papers printed was audited, many papers, however, were being destroyed. I felt sick. The effect of all this on my selling ability was devastating. I became more and more immobile; after a few months I would stare at the walls, or when in public contact, would apologize when anyone bought an ad. At the end of the fourth month, my employer and I met in the hall: I said, "I quit"; and he said, "You're fired." It was a relief for both of us.

The advertisers who support my current publication would probably tell anyone that I am an absolute steamroller of persistence for sales. They would say so because when I obtain a client's signature on a contract I am convinced that I have done that client a favor. I am going to make that advertiser money.

Fear of loss of femininity

Many women who desire a career are often inhibited by the irrational fear that somehow if they seriously try to achieve their goal they will lose their femininity. They fear that their personality will change for the worse. They fear that they will no longer be appealing to the opposite sex, that they will become harsh and emotionally cold.

Much of these fears can be attributed to the confusion that surrounds the word "femininity." Ask 100 women to define femininity and you'll probably receive 100 different answers. Many of the answers will be vague and confusing, which is to be expected, considering that the ideal presented to women over the years has been not only confusing, but also contradictory to say the least.

Webster's defines female as "a woman or girl as distinguished from a man or boy: syn. WOMAN, LADY: FEMALE is the regular term where mere classifications of persons, animals, or plants is intended but is used of persons only in contempt or derision."

Webster's *continues, "WOMAN is the generally
accepted term applying to all adult female persons
regardless of rank or character; LADY specifically
designates a woman of rank and connotes the
qualities of dress, manner, and social behavior
commonly associated with the women of the
privileged classes. FEMALE stresses the fact of sex;
used otherwise than scientifically or statistically it has
a contemptuous or patronizing suggestion; WOMANLY
suggests qualities especially associated with the ideal
wife or mother; WOMANLIKE suggests faults and
foibles thought typical of women; WOMANISH
suggests weakness and emotionalism and is used
chiefly in reference to a man; EFFEMINATE
emphasizes the softer or more delicate aspects of a
woman's attitudes and behavior and applies chiefly to
men, implying a lack of virility or masculinity;
LADYLIKE suggests decorous, daintiness, or lack of
expected masculine force or strength."*

Webster's *seems to imply that the word femininity not
only connotes an essence of softness, but also of
weakness. In the 1960s the media constantly
portrayed the ideal woman as a perfectly groomed
and eternally young, but decidedly an empty-headed,
sex goddess.*

*Femininity is the invisible essence of every woman.
It's neither good nor bad, superior or inferior; it's
simply that powerful substance that separates woman
from man and in the selling game can definitely be on
asset.*

*The Women's Liberation movement in later years
focused on women's equality. During this period,*

however, women in this movement demonstrated much hostility and rage toward men. It seemed that many of these vocal, and at times almost militant, leaders believed that the only solution for the betterment of women was that men be either totally eliminated or at least dominated. At best, the impression was given that women could only gain equality when all differences between the sexes ceased to be acknowledged or recognized.

It is little wonder that many women are confused regarding their femininity and what it actually means. Years ago a woman could only be assured of a few things. She was expected to bear and nurture children and act as a helpmate of her husband. She was literally either her father's or her husband's possession. Women were often viewed as lesser human beings and even, in extreme cases, were viewed as evil and weak creatures who needed to be controlled. Women were often the pawns of economic and political alliances. In ancient Persia women's social standing was so low that they were of lesser value than the livestock. In Arabia it is possibly still believed that to look deeply into a woman's eyes is to risk losing one's chance to enter paradise. In the Victorian era a woman was either put on a pedestal where she was regarded as an innocent and simple creature much in need of protection or she was labeled wanton.

Yet, throughout history, when things literally fall apart—it is often the woman who picks up the pieces and gets the cycle of life back in motion. Most women have no idea of their inner strength and endurance. Instinctively, a woman knows that she will go to almost any length to feed and protect her children and those she loves. Throughout the years women have operated on an emotional level and when the chips are down her incredible strength comes to the foreground. She buries her dead, bandages up the wounded, bears her young, and goes about the business of living.

Throughout the years women have survived through skillful diplomacy, patience, and cleverness. These traits have made the woman a skillful manipulator and are possibly the basis for the hidden fear that many men have of women. These same traits when used in a positive manner also make her a candidate for success in sales.

It is important that any woman entering a career in business gain a proper perspective of her femininity. She should know what it means and how it can be used. Femininity does not necessarily mean weakness or seduction. It does mean that there will be some people in her career who will react to her in a negative manner because she is female. Not all these people will be men—some will be women. Some men will be unwilling to acknowledge her intelligence or give credit to her ideas. Some women will look at her as potential competition and treat her as a rival. Fortunately, there will be many others who feel secure enough to embrace such women and gain valuable friends and allies.

Much is to be said for the strength of the female if she has a positive and healthy attitude toward herself and others. Until this time in our history few women have had the opportunity to be successful in business.

Women were usually the victims of their times—but even then many of them provided the strength their families needed to survive.

Case

A century ago there was a young woman whose father was a most vain and extremely opinionated Prussian. Typical of his era and nationality the man totally dominated his family. His tyranny was even more pronounced because he felt, and indicated to everyone who would listen, that he had married beneath him. He referred to his wife as a black German—a product of peasant stock. This proud man's problem was that he found himself in America with no money. His bloodlines and family name meant nothing. He was cagey in his selection of a wife. He picked a woman who was physically very strong and who had an overabundance of good nature and humor. She was not at all pretty and was in awe of her handsome husband. Naturally, she and the children she bore from this union did most of the farm work. The daughter, Marie, in many ways resembled her mother. She was fiercely independent and demonstrated a terrible temper when pushed too far. She never accepted the fact that she was of less value than anyone. When in her teens she committed the unforgivable. She entered a racially unacceptable marriage. Her husband was Polish and everyone knows that the Germans hate the Poles. Her father never forgave her. Her father not only hated the Poles, he hated the Russians, Italians, the French, and the Indians. On the day of her wedding, Marie found herself totally cut off from her family.

Years later Marie's husband died while trying the rescue a man from a well that was leaking sour gas. Marie's fourth child was born a few weeks later and she found herself totally on her own with four children to support. She sold her possessions, took her children, and migrated to Montana where she was pushed further and further north in search of land that was not already taken. She settled just south of the Canadian border where she dug her own root cellar and eventually remarried. Until that time she and her children existed on a $75 monthly pension provided to widows of heroes through a Carnegie fund. She farmed and she worked. She cooked for a small rural school and weathered many a fierce storm to get back and forth to the school. At the school she hauled her own water and baked bread. She became an avid nutritionist. Many of the children who enrolled in the fall were frail and underfed, but when they left every spring they had rosy cheeks and sparkling eyes. She was fiercely proud that she was able to put two of her children through high school. She is now a very elderly lady loved by all—she is my grandmother.

This story has absolutely nothing to do with sales, but it does demonstrate the inner strength of the female when she is put in a position where she must survive. Hopefully, this woman instilled in me some of the virtues that contribute to my success today.

My father's mother Margaret Parkhurst comes from a totally different background; yet her story is just as impressive.

Case

Margaret Parkhurst married a man who was a Parkhurst, supposedly a direct descendant of English nobility. Being poor, however, his name was of no value whatsoever. My father's mother has worked all of her life. Her husband became an invalid and she assumed the role of provider for her family. She did this with an attitude of kindness and dignity. She nursed her husband until his death, reared two boys, and weathered the depression. There was one period in her life when within one year she went from selling expensive garments to wealthy ladies in a leading department store in Chicago to felling trees and clearing brush in a forest in Wisconsin. She looks back on these times with humor and does not feel that life has mistreated her in any way.

An avid photographer, she has numerous albums of photos. During the racial riots in Washington, D. C., during the 1960s she stood on the roof of her building calmly taking pictures. Had she been born at a later age, she probably would have been a commercial photographer. But in her youth such an idea was unthinkable.

Most of you have parents, grandparents, or relatives similar to mine who have demonstrated strength and determination overcoming tremendous obstacles. The endurance and willingness of your parents and mine to work hard and take risks have made the life-styles possible that we now enjoy. Let us take these characteristics and use them to our advantage. To be successful in sales one must work hard, be willing to dare, and have faith and endurance.

I realize that many people after reading this may groan and silently think, "Oh God, not one of those old pioneer stories again!" My point is simply this: If the chips are down women would find themselves shocked at just how hard working and daring they could be. Few of us are conscious of how tough we are. Our ancestors had adversity as a testing ground. In our mechanized society we are privileged and find it necessary to discover our internal strengths in other ways.

Women often confuse aggressiveness with assertiveness. They assume that to be successful in business they must be overbearing and belligerent. Many women in striving for promotion demonstrate an unwarranted rivalry between themselves. I'm constantly told by women that they do not trust or like other women. This statement, to me, is a dangerous signal that spells insecurity. A woman who is secure within herself can afford to make friends and build alliances with other executives, whether they be male or female. She does not need to worry about others; she simply needs to set her goals and move straight ahead. The way a woman conducts herself, her attitudes, and her characteristics can all enhance her femininity.

Case
Ann exemplifies a woman who has retained her femininity while success-

fully competing in a male-dominated field. She was in my evening class — a course for women who wanted a selling career or who wanted to polish their selling skills. She sold electrical equipment for the telephone company. I was intrigued by her job and wanted to know more. She recalled that when she was hired there had been some snickers and comments from her male co-workers, but within six months they were her friends, and allies. How did she do it? She didn't do it by playing little girl games or taking a defensive or belligerent attitude. The salesreps had to carry heavy cases, which she did and never expected assistance. She did not demand concessions or special favors because she was a woman. When she was criticized for something, she responded logically without throwing tantrums or bursting into tears. She was willing to learn. She worked as hard, if not harder than the others. Yet she is an ultrafeminine woman. The last I heard about her, she still enjoyed her job and was making excellent money. She had just gone on a great vacation with her husband who is justifiably proud of her and her achievements.

To choose
or not
to choose

Some women are afraid that if they wholeheartedly
enter a career they will be forced to make a choice
between it or a mate. I have been in this position and
have seen others struggle with it. What many of us
fail to understand, until it is too late, is that there
doesn't need to be a choice.

The male with a healthy ego is not threatened by
women. He doesn't want to be saddled with a
helpless, simpering wife. If a man is successful and
content within himself, he will admire his wife's or
girlfriend's ambition. He'll encourage her and be
interested in her endeavors. If he is also ambitious
they will have much to share and gain a mutual
respect and understanding.

Unfortunately, not everyone is this mature. People
tend to be ruled by emotions. No matter our age,
many of us have our hang-ups and are emotionally
immature. Often the relationship between a man and
a woman begins beautifully. Sadly, if each partner is
not emotionally mature the relationship can become
one in which one partner dominates or where they
spend most of their time manipulating each other.
When faced with a choice between a career or a

*relationship with a man, the aspiring businesswoman
often fails to realize that the answer is logically clear-
cut. If she chooses the man over a career, she ends up
years later with a broken relationship and the wishful
fantasies of what she could have been.*

*I have seen the outcome of women who faced these
dilemmas. I have watched young women enter my
organization, flash upward on the scale of success,
and then fade away leaving behind only the
frustrations of knowing what they might have been.*

*These young women enter with shining eyes, receptive
natures, and a gung-ho attitude. They are loaded with
optimism. Everything is fine at first. They work hard,
their sales grow, and they have a marvelous time.
Then they get into a relationship and become
engaged. The job performance of these women
gradually deteriorates. They try to burn the candle at
both ends. Our starry-eyed young career woman is in
love and her lover is dazzled. She feels she must keep
him dazzled. She meets his every whim. She helps
entertain his clients, throws elaborate dinners for his
friends, spends a lot of time with his family, and stays
out late night after night. She rushes round pell-mell,
trying vainly to be the woman of his dreams and an
efficient worker besides. Inevitably, something must
give. Usually, it's the woman's job. She begins to come
in later and later and call in less and less. Then she
begins to miss commitments and then a deadline—the
ultimate sin in publishing. Self-discipline is one of the
most important aspects of being a success in sales. No
matter how charming, bright, or magnetic you are,
without self-discipline you will not be a success in
sales.*

CASE:
My friend Marsha illustrates what happens when one chooses love over a career. Pretty, extremely charming, and forceful, she has everything going for her. She should be well into a good sales career, but she hasn't even reached first base and she has had many opportunities. Her manner is so impressive that when she walks in an employer's door she makes an astounding impact. If the firm is large, this young saleswoman is tested and always scores in a high bracket. It is not unusual for her to be offered a job on the spot. Yet when she takes a job she rarely lasts six months. Why? She is always on some man's string. She is an emotional victim of whatever man she is involved with. I watched how Marsha conducted her life when she was single and I'm watching how she does so while married. Her husband, Ken, is an obsessively driven businessman. I've no doubt that he will be a big success someday in business, but not in the handling of his personal relationships, which are treated questionably. Marsha is in a no-win relationship; she quit the best job of her entire life because he did not want her to travel. She keeps the house and pays for all of the incidentals, luxuries, utilities, and groceries. Fortunately she has an independent source of income.

Marsha's life revolves around her husband. Ken works late hours and weekends. She is always there. Yet, he deeply resents any dependency financially that she might have on him, which at this point is none. He complains about paying the rent. When they go out for dinner with friends, he complains when he pays for the drinks. If she has a good time, he sulks. He takes out all of his frustrations on her. This couple's life has settled into a monotonous pattern. Four weeks pass beautifully and then for two weeks her life is miserable. Each battle leaves Marsha a little more weary and a little more disillusioned. She is kindhearted and innocent, but someday she will leave this situation and wonder where she would be if she had not quit that job where she was paid so well and traveled. She made a choice that did not work out.

If Marsha had chosen to keep her job, demanded that her husband share their mutual responsibility, and allowed him to make the choices, perhaps he would have matured and developed a better self-image. If he never matured, as all this suggests he did not, then surely Marsha could get someone else in her life who appreciates and respects her for the marvelous person she is.

I'm not saying that we should all be totally self-sufficient and cold-blooded in our relationships. We are all dependent to some extent. We all need love and we all need to feel that we can count and rely on someone. Marsha married a man she thought could give her the love and emotional support she needed. She very much wanted the security of marriage. Her dilemma, like many such cases, is ironic. She has no security. Her husband constantly worries and complains. She pays more than her share financially; yet her contribution is never recognized. He is terribly jealous of her and does not want her to work. She finds herself in a no-win position.

Men constantly refer to me as being extremely independent. I find this amusing. If there was anyone less suited for emotional independence years ago, it was me. I will say, though, that my most outstanding characteristics are my tenacity and will to survive.

As I see it, we can choose our actions, but we cannot choose the consequences of those actions. A romanticist, I am all for love, but when "love" means continually putting yourself last and constantly losing instead of winning, then this to me is not love; it's masochism.

Women versus little girls

There is an old saying that within every little girl is the potential woman and that within every woman is a little girl. What separates the woman from the little girl? The answer is the same characteristics that contribute to a woman's (and man's) success in sales: self-confidence, mental toughness, ambition, and the willingness to work hard. The lack of these traits is the undoing of the little girl.

For the adult woman who remains a perpetual child, these qualities will always remain out of reach. Why? Because the little girl (and I am amazed at the vast number of little girls running around in grown women's bodies) spends her entire life playing little girl games: she's cute and adorable, she's in a soap opera, she's poor little me, she's seductive, she's a spoiled child, and she has temper tantrums. More will be presented about these games later.

We all harbor a little girl within ourselves. She's our inner child and she is responsible for the bounce in our walk, the sparkle in our eyes, and she definitely enhances our femininity. Without the little girl within us we would be dull, lifeless company, indeed. But the *mature woman is able to keep her inner child firmly in check until playtime. Each woman's life is ruled by her state of maturity, which has nothing to do with her age. By developing the necessary characteristics for success the woman's potential in sales is great. She will enjoy financial reward, she will be goal oriented, self-sufficient, and fulfilled.*

The little girl, on the other hand, is perpetually insecure. A skilled manipulator, she lives in a fantasy world and conducts her life in a perpetual soap opera fashion. It's not unusual to find the little girl dissatisfied with life in general. Most certainly, she is a disaster in sales.

The little girl masquerading in a woman's body is eternally unhappy. She is so unsure of herself that she can never truly maintain a belief in anything or anyone. She is like a leaf that drifts from place to place in the wind. Her lack of belief and lack of self-confidence results in confusion and fear. She can be like a mirror reflecting everything around her or she can be paralyzed into a state of inactivity. Any success that she may enjoy is temporary at best.

Case

Susan had a truly magnetic personality. She loved people, could talk to anyone, and felt completely comfortable in any social situation. The ability she had to influence others and her powers of persuasion were excellent. She made friends wherever she went. She was charming and fun to be with. Yet she proved to be a complete failure in sales. Why? She had such a complete lack of faith in herself that she was unable to believe completely in anything or anyone; she was a little girl. As delightful and entertaining as she was, Susan was my first lesson that little girls do not make good salespeople.

She had previously lived in the South. In her early forties, she was now dealing with her recent role as a single supporter of two children. She was on her own for the first time in her life. Susan's two brothers, both successful in their own careers and who lived in Dallas, had prompted her to move to there. She had gone from college into a long marriage in which she loved her husband, played the role of mother and wife to perfection, and entertained as she liked. Her divorce was prompted by the discovery that her husband was not only unfaithful, but also was a con artist. He embezzled a huge sum of money from their small hometown and also managed to get $80,000 from her brothers. Because of this, she came to Dallas to begin life anew. I met her at a luncheon and was captivated by her charm. I hired her for sales.

Our problems began soon after she started working for me. She started out enthused about the magazine I publish and I was confident she would do very well. It didn't take me too long to realize, however, that I was dealing with a little girl.

My company was new and my staff and I had just moved into our first office. Susan refused to take the job seriously. Her brothers convinced her that my company was not big enough for her. I found out later she planned to stay with me only until a "solid" job offer or "Mr. Wonderful" came along. Despite this, I think she could have made it if these had been her only concerns. What defeated her was her inability to believe in our product. I thought, at first, this would change. It didn't. I would send her off in the mornings enthused and ready to take on an army. She would come dragging back a few hours later expressing every doubt she had heard regarding the magazine. I would patiently relate every success story available, which, even then, was impressive. We had better reproduction, lower rates, and a more personal and interesting magazine than many people are ever exposed to. We enjoyed tremendous influence within the community and produced profitable results for our advertiser's dollar. Susan would sit with a doubtful expression on her face as I related success story after success story.

Finally, it would seem that she was convinced. Unfortunately, she'd reappear hours later convinced our product wasn't good enough. She would buy the customer's objections. When we were compared to a shopper paper in terms of rates, she would come in stating that our prices were too high even though we were a reading supplement with 40 to 50 percent editorial content. She would state that times were hard, the season was wrong, and so on. She became totally predictable. She would get in a lot of selling situations, but invariably she was the one who was sold. We went to the necessary social functions and there she shone. "I bet she is one heck of a saleswoman," one admiring builder commented to me after one party. During my staff meetings she giggled, made distracting comments, and conducted herself exactly like a little girl sitting through a boring lecture. Any self-improvement course I tried to get her into was either not attempted or quickly abandoned—always because of her brothers' scorn or ridicule. I caught her one day answering our business phones with the name of a renowned singles bar.

Finally, I realized the greatest favor I could do her and myself was to let her play her games elsewhere. She was a little girl playing the little girl games of baby sister being protected by big strong brothers; all her efforts seemed aimed at being cute and adorable. She was insecure. She wanted security. She was not able to believe in herself; thus she was unable to believe in her product. She wanted to be taken care of. She did not want responsibility. She had no faith or confidence in her own ability. She obtained a job at a major paper. I introduced her to the man she later married. Eventually, her husband was transferred to the West Coast and she found herself away from her family's influence. She held other jobs and I believe finally made the mental and emotional move toward maturity.

She comes to Dallas occasionally and always calls. Invariably, she tells me that the best job and the best training that she ever received was with me.

At the time I worked with her she was a charming, adorable little girl. And as such she was a disaster in sales.

Selling, as pointed out earlier in this text, is not an inborn trait. I am constantly asked what specific personality traits I look for when hiring saleswomen. I look for character and maturity. Maturity is a must in sales. I have known successful salespeople who had different personalities, were of every age, and came from every sort of environment. I have seen the quiet, unassuming, and average-appearing individual enjoy outstanding success. I have also seen the flashy and magnetic person fail dismally. After years of watching these phenomena, I have finally realized that the degree of one's success is in direct proportion to one's character and maturity. Failure is often brought about by immaturity. Without maturity there is no way an individual can develop the necessary ingredients needed for success.

Industrial saleswomen: where do they come from?

Industrial saleswomen come from a wide variety of backgrounds. But many are from one of four categories:

1. Bored Housewife
2. Secretary
3. Desperate Woman
4. College Graduate

To better understand the women's problems and the adjustments they must make on entering the sales field, an examination follows of each of these categories.

Bored Housewife

The bored housewife is an excellent candidate for a sales job. The housewives who are just entering business generally are intelligent, have good educations, and are thrilled about the prospect of

*having a career. They are determined to be successful
on their own.*

*They often feel that they have been living their lives
for others. They express feelings of restlessness and
emptiness. It's not uncommon for them to be angry
and to claim that their greatest fear is stagnation.
They often have played a supportive role for their
children and their husband's career. They have
attempted to live up to an image of the perfect
woman, which often required that they entertain
superbly and act as hostess, chauffeur, nursemaid,
housekeeper, playmate, and psychologist. Many times
these women say that they are tired of playing a
passive and secondary role in life. They are frustrated
with the knowledge that they have talents and
resources they have not even begun to explore.*

*After endless rounds of tennis, golf, coffees, parties,
art courses, and self-improvement courses, many
women still feel they are bored and lack a sense of
fulfillment. The bored housewife, who is not to be
confused with the desperate woman (a subject for
subsequent discussion) is often quietly desperate.*

*Once the bored housewife begins her career, she can
become totally absorbed with it. She rushes to work
in the morning; after years of cleaning and
supervising children she looks on her new work as
fun. But the bored housewife faces some problems in
the business world. The ability to set priorities
successfully seems to pose great difficulty. Many
women in their thirties and forties seem to have
difficulty accepting that they are not superwomen.
They have been trained from early childhood to meet*

the needs of others. They feel it is their responsibility to keep a perfect house, make certain their husbands shirts are ironed and starched, entertain, be the perfect mother, and at the same time juggle a career. I have learned from painful experience that such simply cannot be done.

Those shirts can be dropped off at the cleaners by the husband, children, or you. Food can be prepared in advance, with help from everyone; and the whole family can also help with cleaning the house. Children usually find themselves able to do more than they realized when mother no longer picks up after them. They thrive on the sense of self-sufficiency and independence. I had one saleswoman who would rush home to do her laundry in the middle of the rush to meet a deadline. She ruined a good career because she tried to do everything. She would come to work tired from housework.

My upbringing stressed the virtues of housekeeping and motherhood. And I still must struggle with my priorities.

When I first became serious about a career I worked hard 50 to 60 hours each week. There was tremendous pressure to sell linage and meet deadlines. I loved what I was doing, but it was physically and mentally taxing. I would go home evenings exhausted and stay up hours trying to prepare big meals and clean house. Weekends were spent shopping for groceries, doing laundry, ironing, cleaning, and cooking. With a nagging sense of guilt, I tried to squeeze everything into the weekend that I had been too tired to do during the week. I firmly believed that my floors had

*to be waxed and if I did not have a spotless house
with my college husband and infant daughter attired
in immaculate, freshly pressed clothes, I felt I was a
failure. Gradually, I began to feel terribly abused and
unappreciated. I became hard to live with. Finally, I
wised up. I began to realize that the only time the
housework was noticed was when it was not done. I
began to insist that the entire family help keep house.
I insisted that my little girl pick up her toys and that
my husband vacuum and dust. I noticed that my
daughter didn't care one way or the other if she wore
a dainty dress or a pair of jeans. She delighted in
eating TV dinners every so often, because I let her
select which ones she wanted.*

*It occurred to me that the house would get dirty
repeatedly, but that a potential sales call was often a
one-time opportunity. As my family and my
responsibilities grew, I learned to turn a blind eye to
an occasional mess. Many a time I have deliberately
stepped over a mess to walk out of the door to work.*

*Now the children have developed a sense of tidiness
and they help tremendously. My husband finds it no
threat to his masculinity to help in the kitchen. In
fact, he enjoys cooking and my young sons show
promise of being excellent cooks. My husband does his
own laundry and I take a lot of clothing to the
cleaners. We eat food that is simply and easily
prepared.*

*We are all much happier. I realize how valuable my
time is and I feel absolutely no guilt about not
keeping house the way I was taught. My income
depends on my efficiency and my attitude, which*

require a lot of energy. Weekends are to be enjoyed. As a family we spend time sailing; we all read, take in movies, go to restaurants, and take trips. We have learned to enjoy each other's company. Because of my busy schedule, my children all have a sense of independence and self-confidence. I am a much happier person and I'm sure a much nicer person now that I no longer try to be superwoman.

One of the marvelous aspects of a sales career is that when you need to be at home you can be. A sick child needs his or her mother. A successful saleswoman is valuable. She can arrange her time as she prefers since she is more or less working for herself. She can juggle her schedule, rearrange appointments, and do a lot of work at home on the telephone.

There has been a long-standing fallacy held by management in many companies regarding a woman's ability to put in as much time at work as her male co-workers. Yet our Dallas survey indicated no more absenteeism among saleswomen than salesmen. Not one sales manager mentioned it as a problem.

In my many years working in sales I have noticed that if people are happy with what work they are doing, their attendance is good. If not, they will come up with countless excuses and reasons for not working.

Another pitfall the working woman experiences when she takes on a career is a sense of guilt about being too selfish. Many women of my generation were trained to put everyone's needs before their own. Once a woman reaches the decision to do something strictly for her own happiness and welfare, she often is made

*to feel guilty. It's not uncommon for husbands, well-
meaning friends, and relatives to insinuate that she is
being selfish. It's all right for her to work out of
necessity, but to work for self-growth and a need for
challenge still seem taboo. I can only state that my
selfishness has brought reward, a better standard of
living, and security to a large number of people. The
greatest reward, however, has been the increased
sense of awareness, the broader sense of
understanding of others, and the sense of
accomplishment that I have gained. By learning to
put myself first in a healthy way, I have allowed my
husband and children to put themselves first. This
makes for true happiness.*

*When the wife goes to work after a long period at
home, her marriage will definitely be affected.
Working can either enhance or have an adverse effect
on the marriage relationship. Much depends on the
husband and wife's maturity and the strength of their
relationship. The husbands of successful saleswomen
constantly express great pride in their wives'
achievement when talking to me. They shake their
heads in admiration and talk at length about their
wives' intelligence and ability.*

*Relatedly, the saleswomen interviewed in Dallas
indicated that they generally received much support
and help from their husbands. We did not find the
home–work conflicts we expected.*

*If husbands are secure individuals, they don't seem to
mind pitching in with the housework, child care, and
cooking. Many husbands tell me, with a hint of relief
in their voices, that it gives them peace of mind*

knowing that, if something should happen to them, their wives are capable of taking care of themselves. After working in business, the wife gains a better understanding of the pressures and anxieties her husband undergoes in the business world. Previously, such insights may have been beyond her understanding.

Case

Sydney was a born optimist. She and her mother had seen some hard times during her childhood and there were times when Sydney actually played the role of mother in the relationship. Her father had died when she was young. Her mother was a soft, rather helpless individual who was blessed with a daughter who was not only beautiful and good natured, but also strong in character. Sydney married a man whose job as a sales representative required he travel a lot. Sydney followed the pattern typical of our generation. She had two children, kept an immaculate house, and did everything she could to be a good wife and mother. Her husband was moody and tempermental, but Sydney was so good natured that she compensated for her husband's behavior and the family seemed ideal in the community.

Sydney's sunny nature made her loved by everyone who knew her. As her children grew older, Sydney grew bored since she had a tremendous amount of energy. She had always loved beautiful homes; so she enrolled in a correspondence course in interior decorating and began an earnest study of home decorating.

Sydney had artistic talent and a superb sense of color. Moreover, there was a practical side to her personality. She had faith in herself and was willing to get out and make calls on Dallas home builders offering to decorate their model homes. At that particular time Dallas was overbuilt. Because of ample availability to building funds, there were more houses being built than incoming people. Fierce competition between builders resulted. Word soon spread that when Sydney decorated a model home, it was sold. She had a knack for playing up a home's best features, bringing in furniture, accessories, and color schemes that the public liked. And Sydney was doing all this during a time when it was very difficult for a Dallas decorator to make a decent living. Sydney's business grew. She opened an interior design shop and was on retainer for various builders. One particular builder found her difficult to deal with, but she wasn't the problem, he was. Her work was excellent and the homes she decorated for him contributed greatly to his success. He found it irritating that he could not control her. She refused to join his firm as a full-time employee; he could not have her services exclusively. He went to great lengths to convince her to join him. He had her decorate a large, glamorous office; then to her amazement, he presented it to her. He offered her substantial money. She, in her own feminine manner, remained firm and he for the first time in his life found himself dealing with a woman he could not control. To his own detriment, he fired her. Her business continued to thrive. But her marriage began to deteriorate.

Like countless other women, she tried valiantly to juggle a growing and demanding business with an old-fashioned husband's needs. He did not enjoy the social functions she was required to attend and refused to go. She would find herself rushing home from a party at 9:00 PM to put the pouting husband into bed. He refused to offer any emotional support for her business problems; he would not condone her business in any way. The more successful she became, the more difficult he became. He couldn't understand why she wasn't satisfied with staying home and playing the role of the perfect little wife she had always been. She finally realized that she had really been acting as his mother and a doormat for years; so she filed for divorce. Is this the tragic end of the story? No. Sydney is extremely grateful that she had her business and was able to escape a negative relationship. Her husband told Sydney's family and friends that she was a spoiled vain creature who was not satisfied with what he could provide and who was taking advantage of him financially. Actually, many of the finer things of life were brought into their home through her efforts.

Eventually, Sydney married one of the custom home builders for whom she had been decorating model homes. They became legal partners in business as well as in marriage; they have recently started a furniture company that is growing rapidly. They have a happy positive relationship based on mutual respect, admiration, and love. Meanwhile, they've made a lot of money and had a lot of fun. They are an unusual and highly successful team. Their success could not have been possible if each had not possessed a healthy ego and good self-image.

Secretary

We've all heard the expressions "Behind every good man is a woman" and "She's actually the power behind the throne." These expressions bring forth various mental images. I envision a strong, determined woman married to a wealthy successful man. His success, of course, is due to her clever manipulation behind the scenes.

Today, there is a tremendous source of power behind many thrones. For the most part, it's a power that goes unrecognized and unrewarded unless revolt sets in. This source of power is the secretary. Many businesses function smoothly because of their highly efficient and knowledgeable secretaries upon whom executives can become very dependent.

The secretary can become indispensable to her (or his) boss. Her services are necessary to process huge amounts of very important and necessary paperwork. Often she acts as a sounding board for her employer, and it's not uncommon for her to become the mother hen for the male sales representatives in the office.

More and more, she finds herself in an ambiguous position. Because her role is supportive, she is trusted. Within a small firm, it is not unusual for her to deal with clients on the telephone and act as a troubleshooter. If she is of a certain temperament, smart, and hard working, it isn't long before she has a lot of responsibility.

She also begins to notice a disturbing fact. She may have as much if not more responsibility than the salesreps (and she may be acting informally as a salesrep), but there is a tremendous discrepancy between the money she earns and the money the salesreps earn. She is likely to revolt.

Case

Financially, Sandra didn't need to work. Her income was a nice supplement to her family's life-style. Her husband owned an advertising agency and she worked for a bottling company. Her boss had become dependent on her. She performed her secretarial duties with efficiency and had grown to the point where she backed him up excellently in sales. Her loyalty was unquestionable and she had developed to the point where there wasn't much she didn't know about the company. She obtained orders from all over the United States. While her boss appreciated her greatly, her role within the firm remained anonymous. He tried to express his appreciation with extra time off, theater tickets, and invitations to social functions. But he never tried expressing his appreciation with what worthwhile employees deserve: more money.

Sandra's husband Earl helped her realize the amount of money she would have earned if she had been a sales representative instead of a secretary. When she went to her boss with the request that she be put in sales, Sandra began hearing the same old story. The company had a policy that prohibited women from working on the sales force. Like countless other women, Sandra was making secretary's wages when she should have been receiving $30,000 to $40,000 yearly. Ironically, when sales dropped, she was the one her boss pressured.

She approached me for a job; I hired her on the spot. As far as I was concerned, her boss's ignorance was my gain. She gave two weeks' notice to her firm, and as I predicted, total hysteria followed. Her employer begged, pleaded, and stormed, but to no avail. Sandra had taken a long time to make her decision, but once it was made she remained firm. She did agree to remain with the company until a replacement was hired and fully trained. Her employer then refused to look seriously for a replacement. He offered Sandra a huge raise. She turned it down. She informed him firmly that she wanted to be in sales, that she wanted to be recognized for what she was already doing—which was sales—and if she couldn't have a sales job with him she would have one with me. She was determined to be recognized as a sales representative and she would no longer tolerate posing as a secretary.

One night, a week later, she received a long distance call from the company president. They talked for two hours. The final outcome was that she was given everything she demanded. A territory, a company car, an expense account, and equal compensation. She called me and told me that because her employer had met her demands, and because she was so attached to her firm, that she had reconsidered and was going to remain. I offered her my sincere congratulations. I was pleased to see that her employer was intelligent enough to put personal prejudices aside and put her in a position where she had already proved herself. Her ability and hard work could only bring them increased profits.

Case

Mary is an attractive divorcee who enrolled in a course I was teaching at a junior college. Mary had gone to work three years earlier under traumatic circumstances. After being a housewife for years, Mary's husband had come home one day, packed, left, and filed for divorce a few days later.

Mary was the mother of two teenagers and it quickly became apparent that she needed a job. Because she had not worked for years, it was difficult for her to find a job. Finally, after much searching, she was offered a job as secretary for men who were manufacturer's representatives for several lines of furniture with showrooms at the Dallas Trade Mart. In desperation she grabbed the job without asking questions. She was grateful that someone would hire her.

It didn't take her long to realize that she had entered a hectic environment. Her bosses were erratic and demanding, but she found that her job helped her keep her mind off her personal problems. And she did need the $800 monthly salary.

Mary is not only organized and efficient, but also thrives on public contact. After a few months she realized that she was working 60 hours a week and becoming more and more involved in sales. As her enthusiasm grew so did her frustration. She found herself literally working two jobs. One job was that of an unpaid sales representative and the other was that of secretary, but her wages had not increased. She had to work extra hours to catch up on her employer's paperwork.

She asked her employers several times to release her from her secretarial duties and give her a sales territory that was being totally neglected. The reply was always the same. They didn't doubt for a moment that she could be successful, but they were afraid such a move would make them look bad in the industry, which according to them, was male oriented and male dominated.

Mary was irritated over this seemingly hopeless situation; she enrolled in the course I was teaching, "Women in Sales." She didn't know how or when, but she was determined that she would someday be officially recognized and adequately paid for what she did best—sell.

The crowning blow came one day when a gentleman from a small southern town entered the showroom and Mary's bosses were both too busy to help him. They told Mary to help him. By using her knowledge, patience, and kindness, Mary was able to write an order for $85,000; in previous years the account had brought about $20,000. She was as thrilled about having made the order as her client was grateful for her services.

Her bosses were grudgingly surprised and pleased, and after a brief discussion between themselves bought her a bottle of California champagne. They offered her no financial reward whatsoever. Mary quit. She was refused a decent recommendation, which greatly upset her. While discussing the series of events with me, she broke down in tears. I assured her that with the ability and performance she had demonstrated, she would have no difficulty finding a much better position. She now has a job with an advertising specialty firm. She loves what she's doing and she's making excellent money.

Case

In 1963 I went to work for a small radio station. It was one of my periods of bowing out of the newspaper business; so I found the new job a refreshing change. I acted as secretary, logged radio spots, acted as traffic girl, wrote radio commercials, and sold radio advertising on the side. I had a great rapport with my boss who lived in and operated from Chicago. I also got along famously with all the disc jockeys. The job was a lot of fun, but it was obvious that I would stay in the same position within the company and go nowhere fast.

The tiny station was under tremendous financial stress, and it was not unusual for my paycheck to bounce. One day when I arrived at work, I found the doors locked; the staff was locked out until the rent could be paid. Another time the furniture was repossessed while I was on the phone frantically trying to reach my employer in Chicago.

I wasn't too surprised when a young executive walked in the door one day and announced that he was the new owner. I was delighted. Everything about him screamed money and success. He assured me that my job was secure and that he was a progressive individual with plans for great changes for the station. These changes began immediately. Not only did our format change (many of the disc jockeys were fired), but we moved into much larger and more glamorous quarters. Within a matter of days I found myself working directly under a very sophisticated and beautiful blonde who was introduced as the new office manager. I couldn't really understand why an office with only two women and a higher-up needed an office manager, particularly when the other woman's only tasks seemed to be sharpening pencils, rubbing the new president's back, and supervising me.

Being good natured, I continued as before. Then things began to change. I was informed curtly one Thursday that I would have to work the following Saturday. Normally, I wouldn't have minded, but my husband was scheduled for minor surgery on that day. I explained the situation to the president and asked why the new office manager couldn't work. I was told she would be out of town and that if I wanted to keep my job I would work. I decided that i didn't like my working conditions, but rationalized that it didn't matter. I had decided by this time that I was ready to return to my old field—sales. I just knew that my new employer would be delighted to hear about my sales background.

After making this decision, I went into my boss's office to let him know of my sales background and to offer him my services. I was stunned by my reception. Carefully, and coldly, my boss listened to my announcement. He told me bluntly that he had no intention of putting a woman on his sales staff. I tried reasoning with him, explaining my background and success record. At least the previous owner had seemed pleased and appreciative of my sales efforts. Again, I was told that the company policy did not endorse women working in sales, but I might be paid a small finder's fee for anything I sold over the phone in my spare time. I was furious. Later, I found that while I had been ordered to work on a Saturday despite my husband's surgery, the office manager was enjoying a weekend vacation with the station's manager.

I decided to celebrate my approaching birthday in a most unusual way. When the day arrived, I marched into my office two hours late. An irate president and concerned office manager stood over my desk. I picked up the birthday card they had bought and signed, thanked them, grinned, and said, "I quit." I, then, proceeded to go where I was needed and appreciated, where I could do what I do best—sell.

I later learned that the station had gone bankrupt and that the office manager had become quite successful selling commercial real estate. Also, the new owners of the station have some very successful female sales representatives. The world turns.

The point of these stories is that women with secretarial backgrounds have great potential in selling because they already have a good grasp of what a business is all about. They know how a company works and they are used to working.

Desperate Woman

The desperate woman must overcome tremendous obstacles and deal with several challenges when she enters the field of sales. She may be entering sales because she doesn't believe she can earn a living doing anything else. If so, she is entering the field for the wrong reasons. A need for money by itself is not necessarily the main motivation underlying a good salesperson's success.

It's not uncommon for the desperate woman to be either newly divorced or widowed and to have dependents. Often she is experiencing a painful and traumatic time emotionally and financially. Thus because of having to cope with all of this, she, many times, is not prepared in any practical sense for a sales career. She may be in a state of shock. She may be angry, bitter, and sad. She probably is just realizing that she has only herself to depend on. Another concern at about this time is how can she survive? She doesn't have the answer; she just knows that survive she must.

This very desperation can drive the desperate woman to a very intense and concentrated effort in sales and temporarily bring her a measure of success. But unless she is able to develop the necessary skills, attitudes, and self-image along the way, her success will not sustain itself. The first test will be whether she is able to put her emotional troubles behind her. It's part of the reality of the business world that emotional problems must be left at home and the work must be done. In business, everything depends on that bottom line—profit and loss.

Case

Janice was attractive, warm, and sincere. People automatically trusted her. She was intelligent. In her two years of employment with me she came up with some very clever ideas for our paper.

When we first met, Janice's circumstances were desperate. She was newly divorced, had two children, and made a little over $400 a month as a receptionist. She worked as a barmaid on weekends and managed a small apartment complex on the side.

Janice came to me for a job. She wanted it badly. I was hesitant because of her lack of experience. But because of her sincerity and because I admired her for her willingness to work hard to provide for herself and her children, I hired her.

No one could have worked harder and learned faster. Janice became a real asset to the company. For about a year we did very well. Then a gradual change evolved. She married and her sales tapered off. I couldn't understand what was happening. We talked often and she always offered a good reason for her declining linage. She was always able to convince me that she had a lot of prospective advertising ready to close. I had originally helped her build her sales by giving her existing contracts of firms that advertised regularly; so with little effort she was making $1000 monthly, which I do not consider good money.

In looking back, I now realize that with her new husband's modest income added to her $1000, she was satisfied. For her these combined incomes were enough.

As Janice's sales continued to decline, I became greatly concerned. I knew that she was not making the new contacts that she claimed because there were no incoming calls for her. When a sales representative is working hard, he or she has several calls daily.

Gradually, I began to put firm and consistent pressure on Janice. Her ability had already been proved; I just couldn't reconcile her performance with what I knew her potential to be. We had motivational meetings and heart-to-heart talks. My husband, who has had many years experience in sales, went out on several cold calls with her on which she did very well. But her sales continued to drop.

Meanwhile, I had hired another woman only to find myself forced to fire her after only three months. My problems with her were completely opposite the ones I was having with Janice. This lady was overbearing and obnoxious. Without my knowledge she was demanding that customers furnish her and her friends with complimentary meals and tickets. She created a conflict with every employee in the firm. She consistently lied. A contract would be established through her efforts, and soon the customer would call saying that he or she would cancel the advertising schedule if she ever set foot in his establishment again. At the time of her termination she had easily cleared $8000 in commissions.

After letting the woman go I discussed the situation at length with Janice.

We sat down and made a comparison on paper of the two of them:

Janice
Attractive, trim appearance.
Outgoing, friendly personality that inspires trust.
Creative imagination that produced tasteful moneymaking ideas.
Kind, warm, and giving nature.

The Other Woman
Absolutely no imagination or taste.
Tremendous motivation to sell.
Selfish, unyielding, and bitter nature. Total insensitivity to the feelings of others.

The difference between the two seemed that Janice lacked the desire and drive which the other woman had in abundance. But I was forced to fire the woman, despite her being a good revenue producer, because she generated so much ill will for our firm. Regardless of what I said to her, she refused to alter or change her method of dealing with people. I now realize that when I hired Janice she was in such desperation that she saw my product as a way out of her dilemma of holding down several jobs and still not making ends meet. As long as she was pressured and generating all her own income, she was able to perform. But when she married and gained another income to live on, even though that income was small, her incentive was gone. One day she walked out of the door and never returned. I had to call her to find out officially that she had quit. Her response: "Please don't be angry with me." And I was not. I felt sorry for her.

Janice is an illustration of a person acting from desperation. She was working for the money because it meant she could survive. But her self-image and lack of ambition was such that as long as there was someone who would take care of her, and as long as she wasn't desperate, she would not make much of an effort.

While money can be a huge incentive, it is not the main motivating force behind people in sales. Earning money through hard work, skill, and wits creates a tremendous sense of gratification.

Some women who enter selling because they are desperate for money undergo very positive changes while they learn their new career. The women's outlooks and attitudes undergo changes for the better. Their self-image improves. This is especially true if they are exposed to positive material and motivational courses often provided by their employers; the woman who benefits from this will probably remain in sales and love every minute of it. She will also become a happy confident and self-reliant person. It is important for her to realize that she must put herself first and that no one actually has anyone to depend on entirely, except oneself. Complete security doesn't exist. And security itself can prove to be a very deadening and dangerous blanket that prevents us from reaching out and experiencing growth and self-improvement.

Desperation experienced early in life often helps one develop into a mature person. People who are sheltered from the world's hard realities in their younger years often cannot deal with the financial realities of the world when forced to do so later in life.

Case

The Taylors were neighbors of mine. Tom Taylor was a kind, helpful man who was always there when you needed him. He was always ready with a cheerful hello; yet he had a special talent for minding his own business. He kept his home and yard immaculate. When we happened to meet each other our talks were always enjoyable. He was always excited about a current project. I never knew of a time that he was not enrolled in some evening course. It appeared that he never grew tired of learning. His wife Alice was of an entirely different personality. She was rarely seen outside her home. She was overweight, and I suspect she disliked physical exercise and housework as much as I do.

Alice was a sweet person. Occasionally, I dropped in to see her for a brief chat. I would often find myself staring at a very formal picture that hung on the wall in her living room. It was an old pastel photograph in an elaborate gilt frame of a young black-haired beauty who had a dreamy far-off gaze in her eyes. It was Alice.

Although Alice didn't go out much, she had a keen interest in people. She could always tell me who was getting a new pool, who was recently divorced, who was getitng married, and who had recently died. She was never malicious in her manner of relaying these facts. She always announced information in a detached matter-of-fact manner.

According to her, her biggest trauma in life was the birth of her child. She assured me that she made sure this mistake was never repeated. Although she loved her daughter, she had not been prepared for pain. She acted as if she had been totally deceived about what to expect and had never forgiven the deception. And no doubt she had been unprepared for the realities of childbirth. Still, I was secretly amused.

When we moved, I soon forgot the Taylors. A few years later I was told that Tom Taylor had died suddenly of a heart attack. After hearing this, I visited Alice unannounced. When I arrived, while standing on the porch, I noticed through the window that Alice was sitting alone in the shadows. I stood there several minutes before ringing the bell. When she came to the door she seemed delighted to see me and soon seemed her old self as she related all the happenings in the neighborhood. After listening carefully for a while, I finally asked: "But Alice, what about you? What will you do now?"

After a brief silence she confided that her daughter and friends wanted her to find a part-time job so she would not be so lonely. She explained to me how afraid she was during the nights. She also felt she had been taken advantage of at the time of Tom's death by an accountant. She stated that until Tom died she had known nothing of their finances. She kept all her incoming bills neatly laid out on the dining room table in order not forget to pay them.

"Is there anything you would like to do?" I asked.

After a brief pause, she answered uncertainly, "Well, I did at one time enjoy playing bridge." She confided that she would like to remarry, but didn't know where she would meet anyone since she rarely went out. We discussed my teenage daughter who is very ambitious. "That's good," Alice stated heatedly. "Tell her it just doesn't pay to sit back and do nothing. No one should end up like me."

As I rose to leave I had a sudden inspiration. "Alice, why don't you check and see if you could put in for a few hours at the library? It's just up the street and I know how much you enjoy reading."

Her face brightened. "Thank you — what a good idea," she replied.

Over the years I have thought back over that visit and I remember the sadness and disappointment etched so clearly in Alice's face. I remember the growing gloom of the house and I think of the picture of the beautiful young girl staring wistfully out into space and I feel sad. Alice was completely sheltered—so much so that Tom was her total security. To the neighbors and the rest of the world she had an ideal life—someone was always there to protect and care for her. How much better for her if at some time earlier in her life she could have experienced a little desperation that would have better prepared her to deal with her later desperation.

The College Graduate

Most often she's young, attractive, and brimming with self-confidence. She has a better understanding of her own self-worth and is more apt to have a better self-image than her older sister. The college woman may also be free of the negative image associated with sales. In her world, she recognizes the highly professional standards that a sales career requires. It's not unusual for her to have a career as her primary goal whereas her older sister's primary goal in life was probably marriage. The college woman is motivated by the promise of intellectual growth, challenge, and a desire for an excellent income. She assumes that she will be accepted as an equal in any working situation and she expects the same opportunity for advancement as her male peers. She often projects enthusiasm and self-assurance. Fortunately, she is not usually hampered by feelings of inadequacy, inferiority, and worthlessness. Her education and attitude help her get off to a bigger and better start than women lacking the same.

If the college woman is from a sheltered background, she may be extremely idealistic. Because of her idealism, she may find the cold, hard realities of the business world extremely difficult to cope with. It's not uncommon for her to have a glamorous, unrealistic fantasy about what a sales career is all about. When she first enters sales, she is often shocked to find herself required to perform tasks she may consider beneath her. Some of these tasks may seem like downright drudgery, since much of her training has been on intellectual achievement. It takes more than brains to be a success in the business world. It may be difficult for her to understand the importance of profit and budgets. She may be so self-confident that she finds it difficult to accept authority or advice. Dealing with customers, mending fences, coping with different people, and tough negotiating are all part of sales. Patience is one characteristic necessary for survival. Self-discipline is another. The college woman may find that rarely does one spring to the top of the ladder of success. Instead, one usually climbs slowly and painfully up every rung, occasionally slipping one or two in the process.

Case

Candice is an attractive, intelligent young woman of 25. She has an MS in English and she is from a very fine family. I was immediately impressed with her when she approached me for a job. She informed me that she had already proved herself in sales with another publication. I was shocked when informed of the publication she had been with, knowing that their reputation was poor and their product was pathetic. She seemed far too sophisticated to work for such a place. (I felt that if she could sell that product she could sell anything.)

At this time my publication lacked a concentrated effort on fashion. She suggested that along with her sales efforts she write a fashion column. I asked for a writing sample, which she immediately furnished. I was impressed. She seemed to be an authority concerning the fashion industry; so I hired her on the spot.

After accompanying her on a few sales calls, I was assured that she did indeed know what she was doing, and it appeared that she would not require much supervision. We plotted the column; I became tremendously excited and immediately decided to go to great lengths with an abundance of space and photography, an expensive proposition. I gave Candice a list of prospective clients, lined up a photographer, and left on a long-planned, two-week tour out of the country, confident that she had everything well under control.

On my return, I discovered that not only had Candice not produced the column, but also that she had only been in the office twice during my absence. She had not sold any advertising. My secretary told me that the two times she had made an appearance, she had been accompanied by a boyfriend who was absent without leave from the navy.

I told Candice that I was very disappointed to which she tearfully responded by assuring me that things would change. She said she just did not have the confidence to take on such a large undertaking. She said she needed more training after all.

Then our troubles began in earnest. We would discuss at length the slant needed for the column and I would give her a list of prospects she should call on. No advertising materialized and what she wrote as editorial matter was actually full-page written ads for fashion stores that refused to support our paper with paid advertising. Candice was spending an exorbitant amount of money to have huge glossy black and white photos of fashions mounted and given to her clients. I told her repeatedly that we were a small paper with a very limited budget; however, any appreciation of this fact seemed beyond her comprehension. I kept stressing to her that we had access to very reliable and interesting fashion material from the Dallas Apparel Market Center. The paper, although small, is well read and has earned a position of respect and dignity in the community. In her charming and poised manner, she would agree with me, and I would think the matter settled. I was dismayed to find more unauthorized bills signed by her and more editorial layouts entering the artroom for people who refused to support the paper.

Then the complaints began. Candice would make appointments with people and then not appear. These people would then call me at the office. When I confronted her she would invariably contend that it was a misunderstanding or that they were not telling the truth. Our retail advertisers began to complain. I was shocked in one instance when Candice appeared as a model in three of the photos in a layout. The photographer complained that she consistently wasted his time. She found it impossible to meet deadlines. Finally, she admitted to me that she did not like selling; she felt it was beneath her. It enraged her when she asked for an advertising contract and was refused. She felt that the prospect owed it to her.

The breaking point came when she turned in a two-page spread on a western wear store I had told her repeatedly not to feature. I discovered that she had hired outside photographers without my knowledge. When I demanded that she rewrite the column, she haughtily informed me that I was to omit it since I refused to do it as she wanted. Now this I found amusing. I was the publisher. I wrote the paychecks. I terminated her. And she was, of course, very upset.

She told me that she was terribly disappointed with my preoccupation with money, calling me a dominating woman and a capitalist.

Candice is a beautiful young talented person. Unfortunately, she has not developed the necessary characteristics that are needed for a successful career. I had neither the time nor the money to wait for her to develop the proper attitudes. She rejected direction and refused to acknowledge my experience and wisdom in the areas in which we were working.

Another young lady—Sandy—I hired not too long after she graduated from college proved to be a profitable, charming, and thoroughly enjoyable addition to my staff.

Most loyal to the paper, she takes on any potential client as a challenge and is a hard worker.

But she does make mistakes—usually as a result of two factors: her overly idealistic and trusting nature and her overabundance of self-confidence. Our first problem occurred shortly after she joined the company. She called on a well-established shoe company. Since the company's main office is in Fort Worth, Texas, she went there to make her presentation. Because she was new, and we were on a deadline, the questions that arose in the presentation had to be answered over the telephone. She brought in a good order. I scanned it, congratulated her, and proceeded with my work. What I did not realize until later was that she had allowed herself to be maneuvered into accepting terms on the contract that were very bad for my company financially. The contract stated that the client had an entire year to pay a one-time promotion that involved a lot of full-color photography and expenses on our part.

Sandy had simply written up the contract the way the client had instructed. It never occurred to her to call me before accepting and signing for the terms. The retailer realized that she was new, idealistic, and confident. In manipulating her, he used a technique that I call "twisting." I allowed her to go on the call without me because she was so sure she could handle it and because the client was so well established, having been in business 50 years. I assumed they would be highly ethical. All this indicates that I, too, have much to learn.

Years ago an enraged publisher roared at a trembling novice because she failed to bring in an order. The novice's excuse was that she didn't know if the order was acceptable or whether she could actually handle it. That trembling novice never forgot what that angry man yelled: "Would you rather be fired for doing nothing or doing something?" I was that trembling novice. I will never fire an employee for trying. I will only fire them for refusing to follow my directions or for refusing to work. Sandy's disastrous contract was due to her own innocence, lack of training, and my careless scanning of the contract.

The college graduate has a distinct advantage. She is usually not confused about her identity. She has proved she has brains and usually knows who she is and where she is going. If she wants a career she has no hang-ups or guilt feelings and she doesn't doubt for a moment her equality and worth as a human being. This outlook can put her miles ahead of her older sister who takes on a career later in life with perhaps a less positive outlook.

Games women often play that do little for success in selling

Throughout, we've mentioned some of the games that some women play that subsequently interfere with their success. In fact, several of the cases presented deal with the common soap opera game that seems to be a part of many women's (and men's) lives. Some others of these games include:

Poor Little Me
Seduction
Cute Little Girl

Take Care of Me
Play Child
Chip on the Shoulder
Spoiled Child

Poor Little Me

*She is the only one in the world with problems. She is
the only person whom the gods have frowned upon
since birth. To hear her tell it, that is the way it is.
The woman playing "poor little me" wants everyone
around her to know how hard life has been to her. She
will spare no details—and perhaps will embellish
them just a bit—of her sordid, deprived early years.
Her parents did her wrong, "didn't understand her,
you know." And School also presented problems.
Those teachers "didn't understand her, you know."
Many men have treated her poorly as have her
previous employers. She just doesn't get any breaks at
all. Luck never comes her way.*

*As long as you will listen to this person's woes, she
will pour them on you—and enjoy it. At times you will
be tempted to feel sorry for her, exactly what she
wants. If everyone will feel sorry for her, then she'll
only be expected to do a limited amount of work. She
won't be held to job performance standards. She feels
that she will be less likely to be fired. And of course,
she loves the attention.*

*For that person playing poor little me with you,
consider asking these questions. If all the person's
tales of mistreatment and misfortune are partially
true, ask, "Why has this person been so continually
out of favor with the people around her? Why has she*

been unable to control her environment to some extent?

If her tales of woe are unwarranted exaggerations of standard behavior of people toward other people, she obviously expects favoritism. Not getting it, she cries "poor little me."

Not only is this game a waste of your time, but also it is counterproductive. In essence, she is pleading for a license not to be held to the same work standards as her peers in the organization, which won't go over well at all.

Further, the poor-little-me player wants to make you feel guilty. You are supposed to feel guilty about how the world has treated her and make the proper atonements. Once she feels she has you convinced, she'll let you know what these proper atonements are. It doesn't take long for the person playing poor little me to lose favor with most people. Such a person's refrain becomes all too predictable and boring. That's why she keeps moving around. For as with the soap opera player, while her lines remain the same, she needs a new stage and new players for her game.

A saleswoman playing poor little me even brings her tales into the sales presentation. She will try to involve the customer in her web of touching tales in the hope of making it more difficult for the prospective customer to turn her down. But other people don't like to be burdened with such a heavy load. Likely, purchasing agents will avoid seeing salesreps who continually try to sell on the basis of sympathy. The game is self-destructive.

Seduction

When God created man and woman I'm sure it was intended that they be physically drawn to each other. As long as men and women exist there will be sexual attraction between them. However, in my opinion, sex and business do not mix. But the game of seduction is still played by all too many women.

Most men don't object to an attractive saleswoman calling on them. In fact, she may have an easier time getting into his office for a sales presentation. A well-dressed businesswoman sitting in a waiting room often arouses a buyer's curiosity as we've previously stated. Sometimes it is to her advantage that most men have been conditioned to treat women with respect and deference and will thus show her the courtesy he might not show the male sales representative. However, most people buy a service or product because they are convinced that it will be to their benefit. Occasionally, I hear of buyers in charge of someone else's money who negotiate contracts in the bedroom, but such irresponsible people seldom maintain their positions of trust for long.

At least three forces are at work to destroy the purchasing agent who mixes sex with business. First, the man's superior will likely disapprove when his behavior becomes apparent as it most certainly will. Bosses expect their subordinates to make decisions based on factors relevent to the matter at hand. Second, competition for markets, and also for the buyer's job, is sufficiently keen that it would be in jeopardy if inferior goods were purchased. And if the goods are not inferior, why is the saleswoman using sex to sell them? Third, the buyer's personal life is likely to become chaotic, if it is not already so. And business executives who cannot manage their personal lives often have difficulty managing much of anything else. Thus it is not at all surprising that most astute businesspeople maintain that it is unwise to mix business and sex.

Moreover, a successful saleswoman realizes that her competitors are going to be quick to claim that her success is based on something other than the merits of her product. And most women do not want such a reputation.

When you gain entry to a buyer's office you are on your own. Your expertise, knowledge, and product are your strong points, your weapons. If the buyer is smart, he will buy the best product or the best value—whether presented by a man or a woman. I have sold an a lot of advertising as proof of this.

I believe that my product is extremely beneficial to my customers. It's doubtful people would be in business for long if they were not convinced that their service or product did not have a lot to offer. If a woman feels compelled to sell her body to obtain an order, it doesn't say very much for her product or for the way she feels about herself and her ability to sell.

Over the years, the women I have seen fall into these traps have always had one similarity: their sales records were lousy. Their successes were fleeting. They proved failures over the long haul. Unfortunately, during their brief periods with a firm their actions had the effect of lessening the esteem others had toward their product. As far as I'm concerned seductive games do a saleswoman more harm than good.

Case

An executive vice-president for an apartment builder, Mary is attractive, intelligent, and capable. Her responsibilities are substantial, including her being in charge of all buying and decorating. Her professional manner is businesslike and impressive. I got to know her when I called on her for advertising while working in the real estate department for the **Dallas Times Herald.**

While at her office one day, I noticed that she was quite angry. When I asked her what was wrong she told me this story:

Earlier that morning a young woman had managed to manipulate her way into the builder's private office. Wearing a short skirt, boots, and a blouse open to her navel, she had seductively draped herself across the builder's desk and had obtained an order for a large amount of carpeting. Mary was furious. The builder found the whole incident amusing and hurried off for lunch at his club where he could tell all of his friends about his escapade.

In my opinion the carpet representative was unwise. She actually lost all future business. The builder needed carpet anyway. If she had presented herself in a professional manner and had the intelligence to determine Mary's power within the company, she could have made many more dollars for herself and her company. As it turned out, she made an enemy of Mary, and the builder would never take her seriously after that first encounter. This saleswoman never sold another scrap of carpet to that particular builder; Mary saw to that.

Although we live in a society that capitalizes on sex, I think it is much less important in business than is commonly thought. Much of what seems to go on as presented by the media is either distorted or is someone's fantasy. The budding saleswoman must not buy myths or believe everything she hears. Most successful careers that women enjoy have been obtained through hard work, endurance, and the application of numerous ideas and vast amounts of energy.

Case

One day I received an angry phone call response to one of my columns.

The caller belligerently asked me what casting couch I had used to get my job with the **Dallas Morning News**. Before I could answer, the angry young man hung up. At first I was very angry, but then I became amused as I reflected on my work background.

I started my business in my home and contracted for the publication to be distributed by the newspaper. Over the years, I have paid the **Dallas Morning News** a large sum of money, have produced a fine piece of work, and would like to think that I have indirectly been responsible for increasing their circulation. There has been neither time nor need for casting couch games, even if I were so inclined. But I am sure there are those who think otherwise.

When I was a novice, I worked with a young woman in a phone room for a major newspaper. She openly admitted that she had an affair with a top executive. During the time we worked together, I never saw her given any special attention or granted any unusual favors. She was never promoted. I did notice that the favored executive seemed embarrassed whenever we happened to meet him in the cafeteria. He did give her a rhinestone costume jewelry pin that she insisted on giving to me to my embarrassment.

The mature professional woman knows that her ability, her expertise, and her product are enough. The little girl is so insecure that she will play any game at her disposal—including seduction. This is sad, largely because it's not necessary. Relatedly, in our survey of both sales managers and saleswomen absolutely no hint or indication of hanky-panky was mentioned.

Cute Little Girl

When she was little, her mother dressed her in cutesy clothes and paraded her before other people to hear all the gushing compliments about how cute little Annie is. Momma basked in glory during this little game. Little Annie may have been about all Momma had been able to do successfully her whole life; so now she was going to take her bows. Unfortunately, this game has no ending. All through her childhood and into adolescence, Annie was continually told how cute she was. And she probably was cute. She learned all sorts of cute habits, cute impish looks, cute ways of saying things. And she learned that they had very desirable effects. People gave her what she wanted when she gave them the cute treatment. Funny though, Annie is not very cute when she doesn't want something. The act can be turned off instantly. The game is a manipulative technique used to try to gain advantage over others. It is called "cute little girl."

The cute-little-girl technique is devilishly insidious in that it can be so appealing and effective. Many men just melt under the winsome ways of the woman who truly knows how to play the game. Women bosses are not so apt to fall victim to the ploy and are apt to detect it from the start.

One might wonder what's so wrong with a woman playing the cute-little-girl game, thinking perhaps that it sounds like fun. The problem is that the game is ultimately destructive for the person playing it. Sooner or later one is judged on performance, on the amount and quality of work done. The cute little girl wants none of this. She courts favor. She courts privilege. And for a while, she gets by. But eventually, someone asks some embarrassing questions about outputs. Also, the mature women in the organization spot and tire of the cute-little-girl act quickly. They will move to end the game, for they don't want it being played in their office.

Take Care of Me

The woman who plays the "take care of me" game is doomed to failure. She is the clinging vine of the business world. She will latch on to her superior or

*fellow employees and in some way entice them to do
her work for her. She makes her game work by openly
disclosing all her problems in an effort to prove how
perfectly helpless she is. She seeks sympathy for her
helpless plight. In any work situation people do get
tired of doing someone else's work for them after a
while. The mature saleswoman takes care of herself
and her job. While sometimes she needs some
assistance, particularly during the early stages on a
new job, she doesn't make her requests for help a
routine.*

Play Child

*Some people never learn that there is a time for work
and a time for play. Work seems to be something to do
when there is nothing or no one to play with. The
play child is totally irresponsible. You can bet money
on where she will be if there is something other than
work to do. For example, this person will take
unusually long lunch hours if her luncheon
companion is at all entertaining.*

*Judy, for instance, had all the earmarks of a successful
salesperson. She had an excellent appearance, was
intelligent, and could talk easily with whomever she
met. But she was fired. Why? Three days before
having to meet a deadline she informed me that she
was needed at the World Tennis couples matches.*

*The mature person realizes when work must be done
and does it. Play must be fitted around the demands
of the workload, not vice versa. This is simply another
facet of the individual's ability to accept the
responsibility for doing his or her job. The play child
is irresponsible.*

Chip on the Shoulder

One of the unfortunate consequences of the women's movement is that many individuals now have huge chips on their shoulders. Some women walk into an office looking for a fight. If a man offers to open the door for them, they consider it a put down. Let a customer call them "honey" and an unpleasant exchange of words may ensue. These women view all men as terrible chauvinists. They interpret everything that happens to them as another example of discrimination. These women will not get far in selling. You simply cannot go far in life if you're carrying a chip on your shoulder. It's my opinion that the woman with a chip on her shoulder is often acting from a position of weakness. She's defensive, fearful, and insecure and this comes across cloaked in hostility. She attacks! The wise manager who sees her coming recognizes all the signs and sees only one thing: trouble.

Yes, most men are chauvinistic. But if they have the business you want, you'll not get an order from them by making them mad. Yes, there is a lot of discrimination in the world. But then the world is full of examples of unfairness. You as saleswoman are not going to change any of these conditions by throwing a tirade in some customer's office. Likely, nothing you say will change a customer's mind about his personal beliefs. Further, by losing your temper, you indicate to him that he can make you lose control; thus you find yourself in a one-down position. You may gain the satisfaction in winning an argument, and feel that you've won a battle, but you'll lose the war. The likelihood is that you won't change the way the customer thinks and you won't get the order.

Of course, it is important that women should have the same opportunities and rewards men have. A woman should know her value and demand it. If a woman feels good about herself, she cannot be put down. Self-esteem results in self-confidence and a positive feeling of self-worth. If the client is not able to see the female representative as an equal, that's his problem, not hers.

A self-confident, secure saleswoman will often be treated in the manner she expects to be treated by the client. Achievement and reward are tremendous proofs of this.

The more I achieve in my career, the harder it is for me to feel slighted or insulted. I know that when I call on a prospect, I am offering a service and product that he or she needs. If he calls me honey or patronizes me, I usually have to suppress a smug little smile, because I know who I am and what I have to offer. And I usually get the order.

One reviewer took exception to our position that the saleswoman should ignore being called honey. She maintained that it belittled the woman. And likely this is what the user of the term wants. But early on, women salesreps must learn who they are and how not to feel hurt whenever they encounter rough treatment. Men are often called much worse things by purchasing agents who want to put them down. Our position is simply stated by the rep whose attitude is, "Call me what you want, but sign the order."

Another situation to consider is that saleswomen may encounter men with chips on their shoulders. These men are mad at women. They don't like women being in "their" field of work. Perhaps the woman has come into their business and is making life uncomfortable for them. Perhaps some woman in the family is agitating them. Whatever, you will meet such men. The woman caught up in the emotions of the women's movement may be tempted to knock that chip off the buyer's shoulder. But unfortunately, as earlier pointed out, she does so at her own peril. She may indeed knock the chip off, but she'll not likely do much selling. Remember that the major reason for making a sales call is to sell your product or service, not to affect the political persuasions or social attitudes of the prospective client.

Case

Nikki is a cost analyst for a meat processing company. She has gained a reputation for being able to determine exactly the profitability of an item or service. A very valuable talent, indeed, but she feels that the predominantly male staff does not accept her as an equal. She is an exceedingly beautiful Hawaiian. She has complained bitterly to me for years that men build a fantasy around her, but do not recognize her intelligence or take her seriously. She argues with the men endlessly only to get laughable results. Remarks drift back to her that are quite unsettling. One man commented that after a marathon political argument that he thought Nikki was insecure and very defensive.

"They listen to me, but do not hear or understand what I say," she complains. One of her bosses became so confused during an argument with her that he told a co-worker later that he thought she was a Communist.

She is now threatening to appear at work wearing a bowler and smoking a cigar. Her reasoning is that the more she looks like a man, the more she will be treated with the same regard and consideration she feels they receive. This fantasy of Nikki's amuses me largely because, given her bodily appearance, there is absolutely no way she could ever appear unfeminine. She would only appear ridiculous and give credence to what the men already suspect—that she is a little crazy.

Because I've known her well for so many years, I see some of her behavior patterns that she is not aware of. She is entrapped in her own games. She is a rebel. She is so soft and gentle in appearance and speaks with such a melodious voice that she catches people completely off guard.

She is a brilliant debator and can say things that few of us could pull off. I would never allow myself to get in an argument with her. She loves confrontation and she loves to shock. She has spent her whole life exposing the flaw in everything and everyone around her. She loves to topple statues. She is right now in the process of winning a lot of battles, but losing the war.

Nikki makes the people she works with uncomfortable. Their attitudes should be of no interest to her as long as they do not affect her. She is brilliant at what she does and if she can refrain from doing what she enjoys doing best (making waves), she will go far in business.

The point is this: a woman does not have to sacrifice her femininity to be a success in the business world. She doesn't have to become a man.

Spoiled Child

The spoiled child can be male or female. This type is easily identified by their childish ways. They pout, have temper tantrums, and do all sorts of childish things when not allowed to do what they want. They lack discipline. They are not used to following orders or accepting the organizational discipline demanded of anyone playing on a team. The reason that this is seen more often among women than men is that many men have this trait beaten out of them in sports during their school days. Teammates can be physically brutal to individuals who are spoiled. The lad who always wants to shoot the ball rather than passing to others will be clearly informed what his teammates think of his "shot-gun" ways. Tony Dorsett of the Dallas Cowboys decided to sleep late one morning; he didn't play the following Sunday. The organization clearly let him know that despite his superstar status, he was going to work like everyone else or he wouldn't be around for long. Many other people have learned the same lessons as they were shipped out of Dallas Cowboys organization as Thomas Henderson found out. Spoiled children don't last long in such environments. Unfortunately, the upbringing of most of today's women precludes such lessons. Often people just smile and tolerate the pretty little girl who exhibits all of the tendencies of a spoiled brat. "Isn't she so cute." There is nothing cute about a temper tantrum.

Conclusion

We have communicated to you several key thoughts that may be useful to your career. First, know that women can successfully sell industrial goods. Industrial selling is no longer a male sanctuary. Moreover, all the basic economic factors now observable would indicate that women will play a rapidly increasing role in America's sales forces.

Inflation combined with rising expectations for a high standard of living will force most women into the work force just to sustain the household's living standards. And as management learns that women can sell, barriers will fall. Profits pave the road to change. Sales management has some adjustments to make to accommodate the woman on the sales force, but all evidence indicates that the adjustments are easily made and pose few problems.

Second, it would seem that the major barrier prohibiting women from entering a selling career is within the woman herself and not from the environment: it is the woman's lack of self-confidence; she just doesn't believe she can do it. The fact that women can sell will quickly become common knowledge; thus this lack of self-confidence will vanish in the near future.

Third, the woman should now understand that success in selling depends more on her personal character traits than on the possession of any bag of tricks. Success will be enjoyed by those women who are mentally tough and who have the commitment and motivation to be successful.

Finally, the woman is warned against playing many of the games that women of previous generations have found to be so effective in social situations. Business is not a social gathering despite the ample evidence to the contrary. Fundamentally, business depends on people doing their jobs, getting the work done.

Appendix A

Some Selling Incidents

You can read salesmanship books endlessly, but never be prepared for all the odd and downright weird encounters you will face on the sales job. A customer may demand that you take one of his daughter's new kittens home to your daughter. Or a flood may wash away a customer's plants and you are expected to help with the cleanup. Or you may be expected to act as a crying towel for some mediocre purchasing agent whose boss has given him good reason to cry. There is no end of the situations in which you will find yourself and you will have to figure out what to do on the basis of your own judgment. However, to give you an idea of some of the more common types of problems that arise, we have included the following 10 incidents, along with some suggested answers to them.

Incident 1: The Promising Prospect

Beth Bond is a saleswoman for the Industrial Products Division of National Corporation, a large and highly respected manufacturer of industrial equipment. At a recent sales training meeting Ms. Bond's sales manager stressed the importance of prospecting; he claimed that each salesperson should call on prospective customers as frequently as possible. He was looking at Ms. Bond when he added that some salespeople were not prospecting as much as they should if their territories were to be properly developed. Beth couldn't help but recall that experience as she drove to see Barbara Moore, purchasing agent at Harvey Corporation, a large, well-established company founded at the turn of the century. During the previous few months Beth had called on only one prospect. She justified her behavior to her associates with "what's wrong with just calling on the accounts I now have? I have enough work to do just to keep my present customers satisfied."

The Harvey Company is located on the main route between Beth's home and the sales office. Moreover, a business associate had suggested that Beth call on them for they should be a good prospect for the line of equipment. In response to Beth's introduction, Barbara Moore replied rather tartly, "What can I do for you?" Beth replied, "I would like to discuss your company's needs and problems to see if we can be of any help to you."

Ms. Moore said, "I think you're wasting my time. I've seen National's products at various trade shows and have concluded that they aren't designed for use by firms in our industry."

Questions
1. Exactly how should Beth respond to the rejection?
2. Where did Beth go wrong in making this sales call?

Incident 2: Back Scratching
Beth was making a cold call on a medium-sized manufacturer during her second month of employment with the National Corporation. After introductions the

purchasing agent asked, "How long have you been with the company?" to which Beth replied, "A month."

The agent then said, "I think I had better give you the lay of the land around here right off the bat to save both of us some time. I know your line quite well. I saw your new model at a recent trade show and it looks good. I might buy it, but our company has a policy of only buying from companies that buy our products. It's called reciprocity. When our salesrep called on your firm a few years ago, he was told that your company wasn't interested in buying from us. On the other hand, your competitor, The United Company, buys from us; so we buy from them. They scratch our back so we scratch theirs."

Questions
1. How would you handle this situation?
2. How do experienced sales representatives keep from stumbling into such embarrassing situations?

Incident 3: Drinking Buddies

Beth was waiting to see Mat Gilly for the first time. Her appointment had been made by Mr. Gilly's secretary for 11:00 AM. Mr. Gilly, the purchasing agent for United Nails Corporation, had been sold to for many years by Sam Woods who had been fired two days previously for drinking heavily and calling on prospects while drunk. Beth opened the interview by saying, "Good morning, Mr. Gilly. I'm your new account representative from National Products."

"New account representative? What happened to Sam? He's been calling on me for five years?"

"Sam is no longer with National Corporation," Beth replied.

"What do you mean, no longer with you? Where is he?" Mat asked rather aggressively.

"I don't know. I'll try to help you as much as he did," Beth replied.

"I don't think so. Sam and I got along real well. We took in some ball games and did the town occasionally. I think I'll call him up and see what happened. My business goes with Sam. What did you say your name was again?"

Questions
1. How would you respond to Mr. Gilly's statement?

Incident 4: Better Late Than Never? Or Is It?

Beth made firm appointments to see good prospects at 9:00. 10:00, and 11:00 on Monday morning. The 9:00 appointment went exceptionally well. But because of uncontrollable factors in taking the order for this appointment she arrived at her 10:00 appointment 30 minutes late. She introduced herself to the company's receptionist who said, "You are expected. Go right in."

Beth walked in and began her interview, "Hello, I'm Beth Bond from National Products. I'm terribly sorry I'm so late; I was unavoidably detained."

"I'm sure it was unavoidable, but nevertheless it not only has fouled up my schedule, but that of two other salespeople who wanted to see me. I have another appointment at 11:00. So you have just a few minutes. Now what was it you wanted?"

Questions
1. How would you handle the awkward situation?
2. How could the situation have been avoided?

Incident 5: Freddie the Freeloader

Fred Brass, purchasing agent for the Graf Company, a modestly good customer of long standing, loved to take long and expensive lunches on salesrep's expense accounts. Your sales manager has casually mentioned that your expenses have been running a bit large because you have been spending too much money entertaining. You have an appointment at 11:00 this morning to see Fred. The sales presentation goes well and Fred is very receptive. He is about to give you a modest order when he notices that it's lunch time. He casually asks you if it would be all right if his two assistant buyers accompany you and Fred for lunch. You look at them and shudder, for you know they both are hefty eaters.

Questions
1. How would you handle the situation?
2. How could this situation have been avoided?

Incident 6: The Hidden Objection

You have been diligently been calling on Harry Hines for three years unsuccessfully. Harry is the manager for a very large company in your territory. You are absolutely convinced that he should be buying your products because they are particularly well designed for his application. Moreover, you know that your prices are competitive. You can see no reason why Harry hasn't been giving you substantial orders. Yet you come up empty-handed every time even though Harry is very friendly. You just don't understand why he isn't buying.

Questions
1. What would you do in this situation?
2. Why do you suppose Harry isn't buying from you?

Incident 7: Fire Alarms

It's 5:00 Saturday afternoon and you are basking in the sun, pool side, behind your home enjoying the fruits of your selling efforts when the telephone beckons. It's Big Al, the plant manager at Western Manufacturing Company, one of your best customers. Over the background din he yells, "That Model 76 we put in last month has broken down. It looks like we need a new spring on the ejector. I can't get anybody at your service department and if I can't get this thing going, we'll have to shut down the plant, and you know what that means. We're working 24 hours a day, seven days a week because this is our rush season. Can you help me?"

Questions
1. How will you answer Big Al?
2. What will you do?

Incident 8: They Call It Careful Cash Management?

You have just obtained a substantial order from a new, rapidly growing firm whose credit rating has yet to be established. You have heard that it is exceptionally slow in paying its bills. Although everyone is eventually paid, sometimes the company is four to six months in arrears on substantial accounts. Clearly, it is financing its expansion on its accounts payable. While you know all of this, your credit manager in the home office doesn't. Company credit approval relies heavily on information from the salesreps in the field in cases where good credit information is not available from well-recognized credit agencies. The commission on this order is very important to you and you think you can get the order past the credit manager if you keep quiet about what you know concerning the company.

Questions
1. What would you do?

Incident 9: The Chickens Come Home to Roost

Fifteen percent of your sales commissions from last year were earned from orders by the Electro Corporation. During this time you had cultivated a close association with Max Worth, the company's chief purchasing agent.

On entering the Electro Corporation's buying offices this day you are informed by the department's secretary that Mr. Worth has been transferred to the home office and that the new buyer for the plant, Patrick Poole will see you. On being escorted into Mr. Poole's office you are informed that he has just given your regular substantial order to a competitor. Moreover, he makes it clear to you that you cannot expect any more business from the company. Mr. Poole is surprisingly candid in admitting a personal dislike of you for your past relationship: "For years you've ignored me and the other assistant buyers in this plant while you and Max palled around together. Well, I don't think I owe you anything."

Questions
1. How would you handle this situation?
2. What is the moral to this story?

Incident 10: Short Supplies Make Cozy Bedfellows

Answering the telephone, you're surprised to hear the voice of Helen Rugg, purchasing agent for International Steel, an account you have never been able to sell to despite calling on this company diligently for four years. Ms. Rugg offers you a large order for some supplies that are in particularly short supply nationwide. All your customers have been put on allocation based on previous purchases. You explain the situation to Ms. Rugg, but she counters with, "Well, if you expect to get any of our business in the future, I think it would be wise to meet our needs at this particular time."

You know that to meet her substantial requirements you'll have to deprive a lot of your existing customers of some of their allocations.

Questions
1. What would you do?

Answers to Incident 1: The Promising Prospect
1. Immediately, Ms. Bond had better start asking questions that will encourage the buyer to talk about why National equipment isn't suited for the Harvey Company. A comment such as, "I'm relatively new with the company and want to learn as much as possible about applications and use of our equipment. I'd appreciate it very much if you would show me how you use equipment such as ours and just why our products don't meet your needs." It's time to put the ball in the buyer's (Barbara Moore) court and see what she does with it. Naturally, Beth should be aware that the buyer's stated objections are probably phony. Beth should know what her equipment will do and know the prospect's needs. If, indeed, the buyer's company cannot use Beth's products then she has done an exceedingly poor job of preapproaching the situation.

2. The last point made in Answer 1 is precisely what went wrong. In industrial selling one just does not go wandering into a buyer's office with the attitude, "Finally, I've gotten around to calling on you; now what do you want to buy?" Stop and think. It's rather preposterous to have a prospect such as this located between the salesperson's home and work, yet not have the curiosity to find out what the company is all about. The preapproach should have included a full analysis of what the company does, who makes the buying decisions, who the firm is presently buying from, what is the company's financial strength, and other related information. All this information should be obtained before making a sales call on the buyer. The buyer in this case is obviously antagonistic. Beth must find out why quickly. She may learn with a little investigation that there may be a good reason why the Harvey Company has not been buying from National. Previously, something may have happened between the two concerns. Or perhaps it's just as the woman says, her company can't use the equipment.

Answers to Incident 2: Back Scratching

1. Reciprocity is infrequently encountered, but when it is this situation can be awkward to handle. However, Ms. Bond is fortunate in that the purchasing agent is straightforward in his objections. Often buyers hide a reciprocity objection and leave one guessing about what it is, for not only is reciprocity often considered unethical, but also at times illegal. In this case Beth should accept the information given her, saying that she

clearly understands the buyer's position. She should promise to investigate why National Corporation is not buying from them. If she really wants this account, she will have to ask her purchasing department if anything can be done to do some reciprocal business with this company. If this tactic is to no avail, she is left with trying to sell her equipment on its own merits. If her equipment is clearly superior to that of the competition's, she must build a case and prove it. She must show that by applying a reciprocity stipulation the purchasing agent is costing his own company a lot of money by not using the best available equipment, which, of course, her company offers.

2. Experienced sales representatives keep from stumbling into such situations by maintaining files on each prospective account in the territory and recording such information in them so that succeeding reps taking over the accounts will know everything that's transpired previously between National Company and that particular prospect.

Answers to Incident 3: Drinking Buddies
1. This sticky situation is not infrequently encountered when one takes over the territory of some representative who has been immensely popular with the customers. Salesreps and buyers can become close friends, sometimes too close for the good of both of their employers. Beth is not helping herself by trying to be devious and pretending she doesn't know the reason her predecessor is no longer handling this account. The buyer is an intelligent person. When Beth tells

him she doesn't know what happened, the buyer thinks little of her because he knows she either is knowledgeable of what happened to the previous rep or she is playing naive—neither of which he likes. On the other hand, she can't say untactfully that Sam was fired for being drunk, because this is not a valid reason for firing somebody in the eyes of another drunk, and these two seemed to be drinking buddies.

Beth's best approach is to follow company policy, which is normally that one doesn't talk about why people are fired. Other people have no need to know. Besides there are legal implications that can possibly erupt if one goes around saying that the previous salesrep lost his or her job because of drunkenness. Thus her best response is this: "I think you understand that it would be extremely poor policy on our part, not to mention causing some possible legal problems, if we were to tell other people why someone was dismissed. I'm sure that if you call Sam that he will tell you his side of the story. Because you are an experienced executive, I think you'll be able to understand the whole situation from my boss's point of view."

Next, Beth must begin to try and establish a relationship with the buyer, but she must avoid making the mistake of trying to do so on the same basis of her predecessor. A statement such as "I understand from everybody that Sam was a very delightful individual and he had his way of selling. I think you will understand that I'm not Sam and cannot sell the same way he did. I'm simply going to have to rely on the superiority of my company's products and services.

Answers to Incident 4: Better Late Than Never? Or Is It?

1. Beth has botched this situation; she should, therefore, seek another appointment. Under no circumstances should she try to do any selling in the short time she now has remaining. The reasons are because the buyer is in a negative frame of mind and will reject just about anything she says and she lacks enough time to do a good job. Thus if she can't do the job right, she shouldn't attempt it at all. Beth should apologize sincerely for wasting everyone's time, because she is at fault. She could have telephoned when she saw she was going to be late; this would have helped everyone. As it is she created an unpleasant situation. Most people dislike being made to wait for anyone, let alone a salesperson trying to sell something. Further, Beth shouldn't offer any excuses no matter how true or how devilishly clever it might be. The reason she's late is beside the point.

   As one prospect told a salesrep once, "There's only one excuse I will accept for your being late for a sales call, and that is a death in your family—*yours*." One salesrep liked to handle late situations by a ploy such as this, "I could lay my excuse on you and you know it'd be a good one, for I would never knowingly be late without telephoning you unless it was physically impossible for me to do so."

   People who don't live in large cities such as New York or Los Angeles might find it difficult to comprehend that often one gets caught in a traffic jam on a freeway and simply doesn't have access to a telephone. This is one reason many salesreps have mobile telephones in their cars. Besides, so much business is done over the telephone these days that a mobile telephone in a car makes a lot of sense for industrial salesreps in many areas.

2. One avoids these instances by not making such a tight appointment schedule. One IBM salesrep used the following plan. He said, "I make a firm appointment first thing in the morning and another appointment first thing in the afternoon. There is no way I know how long the sales calls will take. And I certainly am not going to leave a red hot prospect ready to buy to go on to someone else. In my business you just can't make a series of firm appointments, except if you allow yourself plenty of time. Then I use whatever time is leftover for making a lot of cold calls and telephoning other prospects to get quick appointments to fill in my day."

Answers to Incident 5: Freddie the Freeloader

1. At this point nothing can be done gracefully but take the two other persons to lunch. Generally, in instances of this sort, just try to make the best of it. You might benefit from doing so. By all means do not hesitate to answer or show any sign of not wanting the extra persons along or all advantage of entertaining them will be lost. Make them believe that you welcome the opportunity to get to know them. Then cut your entertainment expenses elsewhere.

2. Don't schedule a call on this type of customer before noon. You provided the logical setting for the incident. It is only natural for most purchasing

agents to expect their last caller before lunch to offer to take them to lunch.

Answers to Incident 6: The Hidden Objection

1. You're going to have to get Harry to tell you why your company isn't doing business with him. This is the place where entertainment is often used by salesreps. Perhaps if you and your spouse invited Harry and his spouse out for an evening's entertainment he might be willing to tell you why you are being shut out of his business.

2. Most of the time when there is no valid reason apparent for a buyer's behavior, then look for an irrational explanation. Harry may be buying from a relative or may have taken a bribe from competitors or may even own a part of one of your competitors. But you know well that there is some reason why Harry is not buying from you and it's not in your product or proposition; so you've got to look elsewhere.

Answers to Incident 7: Fire Alarms

1. There is only one answer you can give Big Al: "I'll get on it right away Al and I mean right now."

2. You will get on it right away. First, you'd make certain you knew exactly what was wrong with the machine. If unable to do so yourself, you get someone in your service department to go to Al's establishment to look at the problem. Whatever, no matter who goes, Big Al expects immediate action on this problem, for if he has to shut down the production line you're going to have one very unhappy ex-customer. Most machines break

down on the coldest night of the year or most
inconvenient time possible.

Answers to Incident 8: They Call It Careful Cash Management?

1. Credit managers are not fond of slow payers.
Sometimes sellers simply don't want to do business with buyers who don't pay their bills on
time and if your company is one of these there is
very little you can do about it. For this reason one
of the first things you want to find out when
preapproaching a prospect is his or her credit
standing. If you are dishonest with your own
credit department by feeding it false information,
your career will be jeopardized. Sure, the commission looks big and is important to you. Many
salesreps, of course, take the position of "hear no
evil, see no evil, speak no evil." The attitude of
these reps is this: "I've done my job by getting
the order; now let the credit manager do his and
figure out whether to grant credit. Why should I
help him?" Well, the reason you should help the
credit manager and try to get on his good side is
that you're going to have hundreds of other orders
in the future that you're going to want approved.
If the credit manager acquires good reason to
suspect the creditworthiness of any order you
write, you may find all your orders being seriously
challenged and delayed until the credit manager
is sure. It would be highly advantageous to your
career if the credit manager learns that he or she
can rely on you to take orders from creditworthy
firms. But if you want this particular order approved, talk to the credit manager earnestly about
it. Often, if firms are simply slow in paying, some

sellers are willing to sell under those terms, particularly if they're able to raise the price sufficiently to cover the interest incurred in carrying the account.

One reason it's easy to get a big order from the poor credit risk is that the buyer has been unable to buy from other suppliers because of the bad credit rating. Deadbeats are usually easy to sell to. Why not? They don't intend to pay you. When an order is too easy to get, you should regard that lack of sales resistance as a red flag.

Answers to Incident 9: The Chickens Come Home to Roost

1. This is another sticky situation, but it can be handled. You have alienated the new buyer by your previous behavior and this person is letting personal feelings jeopardize his professional judgment, a trait that will cause this buyer difficulty if superiors learn about it.

   Approach the situation in this way: first, sincerely apologize for your previous behavior, "I know this is going to sound phony and hollow to you, but I'm truly sorry for our misunderstanding. Somehow, I didn't think you really wanted me to waste your time." Then try to cast the new buyer in a professional role, "I'm sorry you feel badly about my neglecting you, but I also know that as a professional buyer you now hold a responsible position with this firm and will not let your personal feelings of animosity toward me affect what is the best product for your company to buy. It wouldn't be professional."

   The buyer must get the veiled hint that his

personal feelings are not going to be regarded as a valid reason for not buying products. After all, his company is a large account and if the business is switched some questions are going to be asked. Naturally, with an account this important you're not going to let go without a fight, which may mean talking the situation over with the buyer's superiors.

A buyer who thinks you're going to take this news and walk away without doing everything possible to save the account is exceedingly naive. Moreover, any purchasing agent who would tell you such a thing is probably not going to last too long on the job. A psychologist might say that the buyer is bargaining for greatly increased attention and favors from you in the future. After all, if he really wanted to cut you off, he could have done so and made up a more acceptable reason for the action. The buyer wants attention, lots of it.

The handling of such situations depends so much on one's personality and style. Another sales rep claimed he would have said in a very friendly and matter of fact way: "Hey man. You know Max and how he was. He was the boss. He demanded attention. Now you're the boss and you get the attention. Isn't that the way it works? He went on to say, "Above all, don't let this guy walk off into the sunset without making a great effort to make friends with him. You may have to do some digging to find out what his hot button is, what turns him on, but I assure you there's some way to do it. The buyer has got to have some outside interests you can use as a common bond."

2. The moral of the story is simple: you can't afford to ignore anyone. The janitors, security personnel, and receptionists may all be able to affect you negatively if they develop a reason to do so. Moreover, the people you treat shabbily today can be in a position to hurt you tomorrow. Thus professional sales representatives are always aware that everyone they meet at some time be able to help them in the future.

Answers to Incident 10: Short Supplies Make Cozy Bedfellows

1. Certainly, when supplies are hard to get elsewhere everyone may want to buy from you. This is why smart purchasing agents try to divide their purchases between all responsible suppliers just so they'll be able to have a basis of buying from them if supplies become difficult to secure. Of course, some salesreps will deprive small buyers of their allocations to try to get big accounts such as the one talked of here. If you want to use this opportunity to get this big account, and you feel you can work a deal with the buyer so that she won't renege on it later, then go ahead. But don't be surprised if you have some unhappy customers—the ones who don't receive their full allocations. Moreover, it has been known that salesreps will eagerly reduce the allocations to buyers they particularly dislike and give the scarce supplies to buyers they favor. It's for this reason that wise buyers cultivate good relations with salesreps. In essence, the buyer's best friends are the salesreps, because a buyer who can't get the supplies a company needs isn't a buyer for long.

Appendix B

Information on the Survey of Industrial Saleswomen

In 1977, I became aware that little was known about women who sold products and services to all sorts of people other than the ultimate consumer. That is, little was known of "industrial saleswomen," although use of this term has caused some people to constrict their concept of the sales work women perform too narrowly to include those women who sell only to manufacturers.

Nevertheless, the study presented here includes women who sell to people other than ultimate consumers, including retailers, wholesalers, professional people, industrial purchasing agents, governmental agencies, and others who can only be classified as commercial buyers.

The first phase of the study was a pilot survey limited to the Dallas, Texas, metropolitan area. The purpose of this first survey was purely exploratory to gain some insights into the problem at hand so that a more rigorous research effort could be undertaken on a national basis on acquiring the requisite funding.

The research design required finding Dallas-located firms that had women working as part of their sales force. Personal in-depth interviews were conducted with all the saleswomen in these firms and with their sales managers. No sampling plan was used. Each firm located was included in the study. No problems were encountered in finding such firms. The initial contact was made on the telephone to the sales manager. Of the first 25 firms contacted, 22 had saleswomen and agreed to cooperate. This fact in itself is most significant. We decided to cut off contacts at this point temporarily until we had some interviews completed.

We considered important to our research design that all the women on a sales force be interviewed so that the charge could not be made that we were only allowed to talk with success stories. We felt that it was also important to interview the sales managers to obtain a cross-check on what the women said, as well as to acquire information on management's policies about having saleswomen.

Largely, what the women said was confirmed by their managers. When they claimed that they were successful, it was confirmed. When they felt they were having some problems, this also was confirmed. The one woman who had managerial aspirations and felt that she should be promoted was promoted shortly thereafter. We found few discrepancies between what the women told us and what their managers said. The perceptions of both parties were in agreement.

Forty-six working saleswomen were interviewed by June Shafer, the research assistant. The interviews were recorded and transcribed verbatim. Shafer guided the interviews so that each woman talked about each of the topical areas covered by the hypotheses.

The interviewing was cut off much earlier than anticipated on the basis of sequential analysis of the responses. The analysis clearly indicated that so far as the women in the study and their behavior were concerned, their answers were highly homogeneous. There seemed to be little additional information to be obtained from further interviews. The results of the study follow:

Hypothesis 1
Women can sell industrial goods. Confirmed. We encountered no failures. The sales managers reported

that only three women had to be dismissed. (Mrs. Shafer felt that there had been two other failures the sales managers failed to report.) In any case, such a low turnover rate is outstanding. Clearly, women can sell industrial goods successfully.

Hypothesis 2
Women were hired to accommodate the law. Refuted. No evidence supported this contention. The managers refuted it, insisting that a woman was hired because she appeared to be the best person for the job.

Hypothesis 3
Women were attracted to selling as a stepping-stone to management. Refuted. Only one woman of the 46 in the study had any interest in being in management. The women entered selling to make money.

Hypothesis 4
Women will be coming into selling in increasing numbers. Confirmed. The sales managers were happy with their experiences with saleswomen and were actively looking for more of them.

Hypothesis 5
Women will have difficulty establishing their technical expertise. Refuted. Not one instance was encountered where either the sales manager or the woman felt that she had difficulty with buyers because of her technical knowledge. Some of the women dealt with this issue by making three points: first, professional buyers know that no first-rate company is going to allow anyone to sell its products who is not technically proficient. Second, all salespeople must establish their technical competence with the buyer; the problem is not one for women alone. Third, by using some easy-to-use tech-

niques the salesrep can establish right from the start of a sale that she knows her business.

Hypothesis 6
Women will encounter resistance from their fellow salespeople. Refuted. A few saleswomen reported some initial unfavorable comments from men; however, when these women proved to all that they could do the job such remarks ceased. Many more women reported that their fellow salespeople were very supportive and helpful.

Hypothesis 7
Married women will encounter difficulties from their families. Refuted. The women reported that their spouses were most supportive and that their sales jobs have helped their marriages. Two cases of role reversal were reported. The saleswomen were now the sole support of the family and the men were happily and agreeably staying at home doing all the usual housework-related tasks.

Hypothesis 8
Women will encounter difficulty with entertaining customers. Refuted. No woman felt it was a problem. One who had to entertain a lot has developed a very workable system in which she includes the spouses of both parties. Most of the other women just felt no need to entertain. Interestingly, they felt that many of their buyers were relieved because they did not want to be entertained. The managers reported that the lower selling costs resulting from this lack of entertainment by women has not been overlooked by top management.

Hypothesis 9

Women will be at a competitive disadvantage with men because of the locker room syndrome and "good ole boy" routine. Refuted. The women did not feel that this was a problem. Some insisted that it was a mistake for a woman to try to sell on the same basis as a man. They said, "Sell your products on their merits."

Appendix C

David King and Karen Levine's book, *The Best Way in the World for a Women to Make Money* (New York, Rawson Wade Associates, 1979, reprinted by permission), includes this little test to see if you are cut out for a sales career. Perhaps it will give you some more insights into the job and encourage you to buy their book. Yes we hope you buy their book too. Remember what we said about your self-development—read everything you can find on selling.

Test Yourself:
Are you Cut Out for a Sales Career?

The following questions are designed to help you discover whether or not you have a natural bent toward sales. Write your answers down, think about what you're saying and be honest.

The answers I've provided are more than answers. They're designed to illustrate the point of each question and how it relates to a particular character trait that will help you in your new career.

1. Do you have a need to work?
2. Do you like to play games—outdoor sports like tennis or golf, or indoors, like card games, backgammon, etc?
3. How do you feel when you lose?
4. How do you think someone who has known you for a long time, but who doesn't like you, would describe you?

5. Describe a social situation in which you feel very comfortable?
6. When you're faced with a frightening situation or a situation in which you don't perform well, do you tend to back out?
7. Do people tend to confide in you or ask you for advice?
8. If you go to the movies with friends, do you often end up seeing something you really didn't want to see?
9. Do you feel like you can "visit" on the telephone?
10. What is your most significant accomplishment up to this point in your life? And how did you achieve it?

Answers

1. It's important to be serious about entering a new career. Financial need can be one very strong motivation. Even if your husband makes a good living, and you're pitching in so you can afford something expensive or better your standard of living, you can count yourself among those who have a financial need to work.
   It is also important for a woman to want to be a success. An "ego" need to work can give a person the drive necessary to be successful in sales. Needing to work makes success much more visible.
2. People who like to participate in sports or games usually enjoy competition, and people who enjoy competition generally have a good deal of self-confidence. An attitude of "self-confidence"

can actually create an atmosphere of trust and confidence. Sports and games also require a high degree of sociability, and a good saleswoman must enjoy people.

3. A successful saleswoman should hate to lose. But if every time you lose you begin to question your own worth, then you're not ideally suited for sales. However, if you use your own failures to insure future success—if you examine what you did wrong, what you might have done better, and what you can do that will enhance your performance in the future—then you're a likely candidate for a sales career.

4. This is a difficult question, but some thoughts should produce a few answers. You shouldn't automatically think the worst of yourself, but it's important to be honest enough with yourself to improve on your flaws. If the flaws that you've listed here included "dishonest or manipulative" then you may have problems in sales. If you've listed such things as "too persistent, self-important, too fussy" then you can work on those problems and turn them into sales strengths.

5. If you described a situation in which you're with a group of good friends and participating in some group activity, then you're in good shape. You're in still better shape if you described a social activity that involves your meeting new people. The key is to think of yourself as active and outer-directed.

6. Everyone is frightened by new situations, but successful people don't let their fear cripple them. If you tend to throw up your hands in the air and quit, you'll have problems. Think about

your past. How have you dealt with problems that arose from marriage, child rearing? College? You may have more gumption than you give yourself credit for.

7. If people confide in you and allow themselves to be vulnerable in front of you—then they're likely to trust your advice with regard to their business needs as well.

8. A key to sales success is the ability to persuade. If you find that you are always being persuaded rather than being the person who persuades, then you may not be a good sales personality. When you make a great discovery (a new show, an interesting trip, a new recipe) can you convey your enthusiasm in such a way that the person you're talking to begins to feel as excited as you do?

9. In many areas of sales, telephone work is crucial. People who tense up on the phone sound entirely different than they do in person. People who are comfortable can actually make you forget that you're talking over an instrument.

10. The most important thing about how you answered this last question isn't your accomplishment but how you describe your role in bringing it about. If, for example, you said, "My most significant accomplishment to date has been the birth of my three children," then you're actually describing something that happened to you rather than saying, "My most significant accomplishment to date has been raising three children and creating an open and loving home environment for them to grow in." It's important to see yourself as a doer!

Now that you've answered each question and read the answers, you should have some sense of your natural sales strengths and weaknesses. Work on areas you think may need improvement; ask friends for feedback. Finally, accept yourself—with your weaknesses and strengths—and take the plunge!

Appendix D
A Short course in selling

The main thrust of this book is to the personal aspects of women in selling. We avoid discussing sales techniques. However, several reviewers felt that most readers would benefit from a minicourse in salesmanship. Consequently, we have condensed some of the main thoughts from one of my books on selling into this appendix.

About Prospecting

The importance of prospecting, the first step of the selling process, is often minimized by beginners. Many good salespeople maintain that it is the key to successful selling. It's that important.

Good prospecting means higher productivity because it allows you to spend your scarce selling time with people whose probability of buying is high. One of the realities of selling is that you spend relatively little time in actual contact with potential customers. A great amount of time is spent traveling, waiting, and servicing accounts.

Many salespeople make only one or two calls a day. If those few calls are not made on good prospects, the day is wasted. Your performance will be seriously impaired if you waste time trying to sell to people who are poor prospects. Let's examine the mathematics involved.

Suppose two people of equal persuasive abilities each make 1000 calls on potential customers. Sally is a better prospector than Harry; she has selected 1000 prospects who, on the average have a 60 percent probability of buying, while Harry, on the average, will only be able to get orders from 40 percent of his prospects. Moreover, Sally's calls were made on potential accounts that were larger than Harry's accounts. Sally's average order was $900 compared to $700 for Harry. Now let's see what this would mean in sales volume.

	Sally	*Harry*
Calls	1,000	1,000
times		
Probability of order	.60	.40
Orders	600	400
times		
Average order	$900	$700
Sales volume	$540,000	$280,000

Certainly these figures are hypothetical, and no two people are of equal ability. Still experience proves that the differences in the potential payoff of various prospects is much greater than assumed here.

Remember for a moment the great disparity in size among business concerns. You can call on hundreds of small concerns all year and still not bring in the volume that would be available from one large corporation.

Some people believe that a good sales rep is someone who could sell ice to an Eskimo—get an order from someone who neither needs the product nor can afford to pay for it—but that is a mistaken idea. Good salespeople call on good prospects and don't waste their time on poor ones.

Frequent use has been made of the word "prospect" in referring to the potential buyer for a product or service. Let's define some terms.

A *prospect* is a person or institution who can both benefit from buying your product and can pay for it. Notice that two conditions must be satisfied before you can classify someone as being a prospect. First, the person or organization must be able to benefit from your product; someone who has no use for it is not a prospect. Second, no matter how badly the party may want the product or how much the firm can benefit from it, a company that cannot pay for it is not a prospect.

A lead or suspect is the name of a person or organization who might possibly be a prospect. A lead must first be "qualified" before it can be considered a prospect. Sometimes the term "suspect" has been applied to a lead to indicate that the name is suspected of being a prospect.

Qualifying is the act of determining whether or not a lead or suspect is really a prospect. To qualify a lead means to evaluate it in terms of ability to benefit from the product and to pay for it. If the lead meets these qualifications, it ceases to be a suspect and becomes a prospect.

Cold turkey canvassing or cold canvassing are calls made by a sales rep with no advance knowledge about the person or firm called upon. Just walk into the place of business and start asking questions to see if the firm is a prospect.

As a general rule, industrial prospecting is relatively easy. If you sell earthmoving equipment, your prospects are earth movers, who are easily located in the telephone book. If you sell a compound for cleaning oil wells, your prospects are oil well operators. If you sell corrugated boxes, just about every manufacturer is a prospect. Sit on the docks of a trucking company and study the boxes being shipped out to learn of their origins; thus you will be discovering local prospects.

One reason industrial prospecting is relatively easy is that many times prospects will seek you. They have a problem and go to some directory for a hint as to who might solve it for them. The Yellow Pages are widely used for this purpose. If someone suddenly needs a cylinder of oxygen, looking in the Yellow Pages under "oxygen" is the logical thing to do. Thus the industrial marketer is usually wise to be well represented in the Yellow Pages. Many times, sales result directly from the telephone call. Remember, industrial buyers can be busy people; they do not want to spend a lot of time looking for solutions to their needs, particularly for relatively minor items.

But let's not mislead you; there are industrial situations requiring sophisticated prospecting systems. Suppose you are a management consultant. How would you locate firms needing your talents? To provide a contrast, let's examine the prospecting systems used by two different consultants. The first consultant developed a philosophy that management changes trigger a demand for consulting work; when a new president or new hierarchy assumes control of a company, the new people would likely want a study made of the situation to use as a basis or justification for making whatever changes they may want to make. This consultant relied mainly on newspapers and trade journals for leads to corporate changes in power.

The second consultant had a different strategy. He had learned early in his career that the obvious customer for consulting was not a good prospect—the firm in financial trouble. It would seem that a concern in difficulty would be a good prospect, but the problem was that they usually did not have the money to pay for the service. Without the ability to buy, they were not prospects. Moreover, he had discovered that it was not good policy to associate with losing situations, because many of these concerns were headed for bankruptcy and there was nothing any consultant could do about it. Instead, this consultant had discovered that highly successful, growing concerns would hire him to study special problems that they were encountering. Sometimes they felt that they did not have the staff to tackle the problem or that it was beyond them technically. These people could afford the help, and their rapid growth had created the needs.

Directories

Just about every industry has a directory of some sort. Usually trade associations compile directories of their members. Some private concerns furnish excellent information on prospects: Fairchild Publications publishes an excellent annual directory with the names of the buyers for each department store in the nation. Anyone selling to department stores would find this publication very helpful. Not only do most directories furnish names and addresses, but often they include much preapproach information on the firms and their officers.

We have already mentioned the biggest directory of

all—the Yellow Pages—but urge you to partake of an experience. Sit down with the Los Angeles, New York, or Chicago Yellow Pages and go through them page by page. You will learn of types of businesses you had no idea existed.

Advertising

There is one school of thought that currently maintains that it is a waste of money for the industrial rep to make cold calls. Instead it is suggested that it is much easier, and cheaper, to let advertising bring in qualified leads and then have the salespeople call on responding prospects. The advertising has located the prospect and paved the way for the salesperson.

Trade Shows

Industrial marketing relies heavily on the trade show for leads. Because of their interest in the goods at the trade show, good prospects will aggressively seek out suppliers who sell what they need. An able industrial sales rep can pinpoint and qualify numerous excellent prospects at a good trade show if she has been provided with an effective exhibit. The major problem facing representatives working at trade shows is separating the live prospects from the idle lookers. It is too easy to get tied up with someone who is not a prospect and never will be one, and miss talking with a good prospect. The industrial rep working a trade show must develop a series of questions that quickly screen out nonprospects. "When will you be replacing your present equipment?" "Would you like for us to study your situation?" Such questions usually ferret out the real prospects.

SIC Numbers

The Standard Industrial Classification (SIC) system has been established by the federal government to classify our economy into industry groupings. The SIC system places each business organization into a broad industrial grouping and then subdivides each major group into subgroups.

These SIC numbers are fully described in the *Standard Industrial Classification Manual* by the Department of Commerce. Each firm is classified by the principal products in which it deals, thereby posing a problem: What about firms making a number of different products? Answer: The industrial sales rep must realize that SIC numbers will not provide a clue to every maker of some goods but only to those firms whose principal product falls within that classification.

Once the salesperson has identified the SIC numbers of good customers, he or she can refer to a Department of Commerce publication titled *County Business Patterns*, which lists by county every business firm by the SIC number. It provides facts on each reporting firm: payroll and employment, value added by manufacture, new plant expenditures, and value of shipments.

Not only can the sales representative determine how many firms in each county within her territory are prospects for her goods, but she also can learn a great deal about the size of their operations.

The Need for Product Knowledge

"I lost my first account today, and it was a big one, too," moaned big Jim Perkins, a rookie salesman for a large adhesives manufacturer.

"How'd it happen?" asked a friend, who sensed that Jim wanted to talk about it.

"I got too big for my britches: thought I knew everything. I recommended the wrong epoxy to them for a certain application and the result really messed up their production line. They booted me out and gave the business to a guy who knew what he was talking about. I found out that I've got a lot more to learn than I realized. I came out of training thinking that I really knew everything about adhesives."

While Jim had been given excellent introductory training, he was still not prepared to cope with the more complex problems that only experience and much additional study could solve. He found out the hard way how vital product knowledge is to successful selling— particularly industrial selling. Customers demand correct answers to their frequently complex problems: they do not continue to patronize the sales reps incapable of solving their problems.

That last clause contains the key idea. It is not so much what or how much you know about the proposition as it is whether your product knowledge can be applied to the solution of the prospect's problems. *Every sale is, essentially, the solution of a problem.* Product knowledge is acquired for one reason: to enable to prescribe intelligently for their prospects—to apply it.

Some companies refer to product knowledge, as "benefit facts", thus stressing the viewpoint of the buyer instead of the seller.

Applications

Not only must you know your own business, but to be most effective you must also know the business of your customers. Experts in sales force management claim that for maximum effectiveness a sales force should be organized by class of customer; that is, each sales rep calls on but one type of customer. For example, Gardner-Denver Company maintains separate sales forces to call on road contractors, mine operators, and oil well drilling contractors; the applications of its equipment in mines bears little similarity to the applications in an oil field. The oil field sales rep must know oil field technology and the problems of the drilling contractor.

There are other advantages to concentrating on one type of customer. It is easier to become identified with that industry, to be looked upon as being a member of it. By specializing, the sales rep gains the image of an expert, and in this age the buyer likes to do business with experts, not generalists. And the salesperson often gets more job satisfaction through identification with one group of customers; interpersonal relationships become more rewarding.

Mastering applications takes a great deal of study and experience. The insurance agent who wants to do a real job of applying product knowledge to the needs (applications) of customers may have to learn about income and estate taxes, wills, trusts, corporation buy-out agreements, and other aspects of the law.

It is insufficient for a computer saleswoman to know how to operate her hardware. She must also know how to apply it to the problems of her customers. She should be able to show the buyer how inventory control can be set up on it and how it will take care of accounting difficulties. This requires a great deal of knowledge of business systems and control techniques.

While much application knowledge can be taught in sales training, still there are many things that can be learned only through experience. This is one of the advantages the experienced salesperson has over the rookie. The only advice that can be tendered to the "rook" is to dig into the customer's business and learn everything possible about the customer's problems. And the novice should keep right on digging as long as she is selling.

Purchasing agents are expert buyers, and it is a truism that "it takes an expert to sell an expert."

An electrical engineer for a steel company was discussing a 2000-horsepower induction motor that the salesman recommended for a rolling mill drive. "What's your air gap between rotor and stator?" asked the engineer. The salesman didn't know. "Well, I have several other questions to ask, but it looks as if that wouldn't get us anywhere. Good-bye."

Many professional buyers assert that the greatest weakness of the salespeople calling on them is their lack of product knowledge.

A purchasing agent for a chain of hotels asserts: *The word "selling" is a misnomer as far as the job of calling on institutions goes. Sales reps who cover institutions should put service first, and their products should help us to perform our own functions better within our hotel. This selling involves knowledge of product technicalities. You'll find that most of these sales reps haven't the first inkling of their own product's technical aspects. Interrupt their canned speech to ask a technical questions, and they're lost.*

As an example he cited the case of the wastebasket salesrep who called on him recently. A wastebasket in a hotel room takes a terrific walloping. It must withstand the shock of broken bottles tossed into it and resist burning cigarette butts. It must be waterproof to keep liquids from oozing onto expensive carpeting.

The sales reps extolled the attractiveness and reasonable price of the basket. "But what gauge is the metal? What adhesive is used to stick the leatherette to the metal?" he was asked. "Would a good squirt of seltzer soak it off?"

Sales rep's reply, "Huh?"

"It's hard to believe in this modern age of sales training," this "p.a." (as purchasing agents are known in the trade) says, "but most sales reps seem to have been told if they call on enough people every day, they are bound to make a couple of sales. Yet the successful sales rep knows her product, knows her home plant and its manufacturing processes. She can quote prices. She can answer questions. She's a walking encyclopedia on her product. And why not? Her living depends on selling it."

Much of the friction between sales reps and professional buyers is due to the reps' lack of knowledge of both their prospects and their own products. The mention of purchasing agent, department store buyer, or chain store buyer to many salespeople is a signal for a wry face. They consider the professional buyer as a petty clerk, skilled in the art of haggling and "chiseling," someone whose digestion never was right and who would not want it right if it could be right. Someone who plays favorites and expects graft. But the person who is really worthy of the name sales rep usually has a different point of view. Professional buyers spend millions of dollars every year; they must know what they are buying or their firms lose money. This knowledge, furthermore, must be more than superficial. Consequently, they lack patience with salespeople who are too lazy to study what they should know most about.

On Planning the Sale—The Preapproach

A textbook sales rep whose career seemed shaky began his sales presentation to me by asking, "What's your name?" I told him. He continued, "What courses do you teach?" With a greatly overtaxed patience and keen curiousity to learn what was going to be asked next, I answered, "Salesmanship, among others."

The sales rep then began telling me about virtues of the selling book published by his employer. Finally he asked me what text I was using. I told him "my own."

The lad quickly retreated in confusion, forgetting about the other books he had to sell.

Had the fellow read a bit about the importance of the preapproach in selling, he could have avoided his embarrassment.

The professional sales rep learns the prospect's name before making the call and already knows what the professor is teaching. Moreover, the salesperson will know the books being used by visiting at the bookstore. The real pro will know a great deal about the prospect's background such as schools attended, teaching philosophies, and outside interests.

Some information can be obtained at the time the rep learns of the prospect while additional data have to be sought independently.

Suppose you are selling Xerox copying machines. You learn of a new lawyer who is opening an office in your territory. Lawyers need copiers; thus a prospect has been located. It's that simple.

Now begins the preapproach. What's the lawyer's name? Where can he or she be located? Where did the lawyer go to school? How experienced is the lawyer? Where does the prospect live? If you can locate something you have in common with the prospect such as clubs, churches, schools, or hobbies, you can use the common bond to break the ice in beginning the sale.

Your objective is to allow you to plan your sale intelligently. Especially, you will use this information in planning your approach. You are eager to get off on the right foot and thus begin the sales interview as favorably as possible.

When you meet the buyer, you will continue your preapproach by observation and asking questions in the early phases of the interview. Thus the preapproach continues into the approach. No matter how much you know about the prospect in advance it is wise to use the first few minutes of the approach to verify the accuracy of your information and to enlarge on it. Some ideas concerning the prospect may have to be revised and the sales plan altered.

In making your call on the new lawyer you would want to find out if the office already has a copier. Next, you want to find out what the lawyer plans to do about his or her copying needs. Then you would try to find out how much the lawyer knows about copiers and what the office copying needs will be.

What is a sales plan? A good sales person plans the sale in advance. You want to focus your presentation on the benefits that are most likely to appeal to the particular prospect. You avoid discussing matters that may irritate the prospect. You plan answers to the objections that the prospect is likely to raise. You tailor and adapt the entire presentation to the particular prospect—something you could not do without preapproach information.

What Information is Helpful?

The information gathered in the preapproach will differ with each selling situation. In industrial selling while the organization pays for the goods, people do the buying. You need to know about both the company and the people who will be making the buying decisions.

Name. Learn to spell it and pronounce it correctly. People are sensitive about their names. A mistake can be costly.

Place of residence. This may reveal something of the person's social position, friends, and wealth.

Education. This may provide a topic of conversation. A college graduate usually likes to have this fact recognized. The self-made person may be proud to have succeeded without formal schooling or may be sensitive to references about college.

Age. Older people respond to the respect they feel is due them. Younger people in high positions appreciate a recognition that they have climbed fast.

Authority. Does the prospect have to ask a partner? Is the person only a front for the real buyer?

Clubs. Country clubs, church, Masons, trade associations, and so on. Very helpful information to have.

The best time to call. Every person has a routine and dislikes to have it disturbed. You will get a far better reception if you call when the prospect is not accustomed and eager to be doing something else.

Outside interests. Many sales reps feel that the most effective way to get by the so-called cold spot in the first minute or two of a sales interview is to discover the prospect's particular hobby or outside interest and use it to promote the interview on a friendly basis.

But let's not go overboard on this hobby matter! Most business executives would rather discuss their business than their hobbies—at least during business hours. The salesperson who can offer a way to make that business more successful may be accorded a more cordial hearing than the person who tries to talk hobbies. Besides, most salespeople are not well enough versed in the prospect's hobby to discuss it intelligently. A clumsy attempt to drag it into the opening conversation is so transparent that it is likely to defeat its purpose.

Information about the organization. In addition to the facts about the buyer as an individual, certain facts about the business are also needed. You might want to know:

Who owns the company?

If a corporation, who is on the board of directors?

What are the business affiliations of these directors?

Do you know any of them personally?

Who has the final word on purchases?

Who else has an influence on purchases? Many salespeople insist that it is a waste of time to talk to subordinates; they prefer to go straight to the top. Others find it helpful to enlist the cooperation of personnel in the lower echelons. Whichever policy is followed, the salesperson should know definitely who has the final buying authority.

Who is in charge of the department that will use your product or services?

What does the company make or sell?

What markets does it sell to?

What is the plant capacity?

What parts of the finished product do they make and what do they buy?

What manufacture processes does the company use?

Do seasonal factors affect its operations?

What buying procedures are followed?

Who does the company buy from?

What is the company's credit rating?

When does the firm buy your products?

How much do they buy at a time?

From whom are they now buying and why?

Is the firm happy with its present sources of supply?

What problems has the firm encountered with its present supplier?

Does the firm practice reciprocity?

Information on Regular Customers

Many professional salespeople keep data books on the people with whom they do business. On each page they jot down the person's name; religion or church connection, if any; hobbies; family; the service club or fraternal order membership; the amount of the last order; personal interests; political tendencies; other miscellaneous items; and the subject discussed on the occasion of the previous call. Few things are more pleasing to a customer than the subtle flatter implied by the salesperson's casual remark, "As you said when I was last here, Mr. Smith," or "I've been thinking over what you said last May about. . . . " The thought that this chance utterance has remained in the salesperson's mind is deeply gratifying to the customer.

A knowledge of a customer's political and religious convictions will prevent the salesperson from becoming embroiled in an argument.

Sources of Information

While you might think that it is difficult to gather the type and amount of information about a prospect that we have recommended, actually such is not the case. People like to talk about people.

Fellow salespeople. It pays to be friendly with other salespeople. Every buyer has peculiarities that are known to the salespeople who call on him or her, and such facts may profitably be exchanged. These hints will come mostly from other sales reps.

Customers. Much can be learned from customers about prospects yet to be seen. The person who has just made a purchase usually wishes to vindicate her judgment by having others buy, too. She is likely to feel she is doing them a favor, so she suggests that the salesperson call on some of her friends. The wise sales rep strives to learn helpful facts from her about these friends.

The source of a lead. The person providing the lead to the prospect should be pumped for information. Develop the habit of questioning the source of any lead at the time the lead is given.

Newspapers and trade journals. Considerable information can be found in the newspaper by noting the advertisements of prospects and getting a general idea of the community interests. It helps to know something of the town's activities and interests when calling for the first time on a prospect. Such knowledge furnished just so many more points of contact on which to establish friendly relations.

The industrial salesperson can establish common interests with a prospect by reading articles and advertisements in technical and business journals, especially those containing stories about, or advertisements by, the prospect. Good salespeople are prolific readers of the trade press.

Directories. Many directories are published that provide personal data on people of some position in practically all fields of endeavor. There is a Who's Who in many areas, such as business and industry, education, science, various states, and America. If the prospect is of sufficient stature to be listed in one of these directories, much personal information on the prospect can be easily obtained by going to a good library. Various industries frequently publish rosters and biographical data of the executives or personnel of various companies.

Observation. As you enter the place of business, many things can be learned. A sales rep calling on a retailer carefully notes the brands carried in stock, for they indicate a great deal about the policies and philosophies of the dealer. You can tell whether the prospect is enterprising or conservative by noticing stock display, fixtures, and the general atmosphere of the premises.

Observe the person's immediate environment. Is she playing the role of the big business executive? The appearance and formality of her òffice should give some indication of this trait. Is she a hard worker? Again the condition of the person's desk and office many provide insights into her working habits. How modern or up-to-date is she? Look at her present equipment for the answer. What do the pictures on the wall tell about the executive? Is he or she sports oriented? Does she smoke? Look at the ashtrays. Is she prosperous? What schools were attended? Any class rings, diplomas on wall, or fraternal insignia visible? What clubs does he or she belong to? Look at the walls or desk. And so it goes; every bit of material around a person can tell the astute salesperson something about the nature of the owner. A salesperson must be a good detective to put together the clues and come up with a composite image of what the prospect is really like.

The prospect. Last, but certainly not least, is the prospect. Much critical information is known only by the prospect; so only he or she can provide it. While some skeptics may question the practicality of obtaining information from the prospect, actually it is quite common to do so. In most sales the sales rep is there to solve the prospect's problems. The prospect wants these problems solved most efficiently and effectively and is therefore highly motivated to give you complete cooperation.

Sometimes you can get needed information over the telephone from the prospect, but more frequently the first part of the sales interview is devoted to extracting it. Indeed, you may have to spend a considerable amount of time gathering information in preparation for the ultimate sales presentation.

You should never be bashful about asking the prospect for needed information, even though it may be personal or confidential. If the prospect chooses not to talk, he or she will say so, but more frequently the person enjoys talking. The sales rep who commands confidence and maintains confidence will be privy to a great many useful secrets.

The Approach

The curtain rises. It's time to meet your prospect, to make your approach. The approach has three goals: to gain attention, to stimulate interest, and to provide a smooth transition into the presentation.

Attention

The sale will go nowhere until the prospect focuses undivided attention on what you have to say. This is a more difficult problem than you might suspect, for the prospect is frequently in the midst of doing something. Under no circumstances should you be lured into proceeding with the sale while the prospect's attention is diverted by something else. Many times an executive who is busy with work will say, "Go ahead and talk! I can listen while I finish signing these papers." Don't do it! A person can attend to only one thing at a time. If the buyer is doing something else he or she is not listening to you: you must first seize the prospect's undivided attention.

Interest

You may gain a prospect's attention for an instant but quickly lose it if she decides that she is not interested in hearing more from you. People's interest in your proposition can be fleeting if you do not quickly give them a reason for listening further. Secretly, the prospect asks, "What's in it for me? Why should I give you more of my valuable time?"

A good approach provides the prospect with a reason for listening. Tell her how she will benefit, what problems you can solve, why she will be in a better position for having met you, or how much money you are going to make for her.

Transition

The third, and often unrecognized, objective of the approach is to lead easily and smoothly into the sales presentation.You could win attention and interest by pulling a gun on the prospect, but you would find it rather tough to swing from there into your presentation, to make the transition.

As we discuss various approaches let's try to watch for this transition or final phase. It is often the weakest part of the approach, especially when it appears strained, forced, or irrelevant to what has just preceded it.

The Introductory Approach

The introductory approach is most frequently used. It is also the weakest, because it does very little for you. You walk into the prospect's office and say, "Hello, I am Sally North representing the Western Tool Company."

You gain only nominal attention unless the prospect is expecting you. Interest will be minimal unless there is a previously recognized problem which you may help solve. Finally, transition is sometimes awkward if the prospect's mental reaction is, "Ok, so what do you want?" Therefore, most salespeople must use another approaches immediately after introducing themselves.

One purchasing agent reacted to this type of approach by saying, "I don't care who you are. I only care about what you can do for me."

Most introductions at the beginning of a sale are of little value as the prospects miss the name and have to ask again or look at a card after they have decided that they are interested in hearing more.

Often it is best to leave the introduction until after a successful approach has been made. Once the prospect has decided to hear the presentation, then a proper introduction can be made.

The Product Approach

The product approach consists simply of giving the product to the prospect. One costume jewelry agent would merely hand the buyer the most attractive item in the line without saying a word. The buyer would naturally look at the merchandise, and if it interested her, she would ask, "Where's the rest of your line?"

The product approach is best used when selling a product that has considerable eye appeal or tends to tell its own sales story. It works because the merchandise attracts the prospect's attention and interest and provides the best possible transition into the presentation. Also people like to handle and examine products; they like to operate them and take them apart. The product approach capitalizes on this urge.

Consumer Benefit Approach

The consumer benefit approach consists of opening the interview with a statement or question that directs the prospect's thoughts to the benefits you are selling. Sometimes the statement is designed to shock the prospect, thus getting her attention and interest. However, often it is simply a question or statement posed to make the prospect think about the problem that you propose to solve.

An insurance agent handed the prospect a facsimile check made out to her for $1000 and asked. "How would you like to receive that amount each month upon retirement?" The prospect admitted that she would like it very much, and asked to hear more.

An offset press sales rep began, "Your letterheads will cost you about $5 a thousand with this press. What did you pay last?"

Shock Approach

An insurance agent obtained a picture of a prospect and had a photographer retouch it to make him look much older. He walked into the prospect's office handed him the picture, and asked, "What are you doing for that old man today?" Variations of this have been employed using pictures of a prospect's spouse or family. The idea is to shock some stubborn prospects into thinking about reality, thinking about things they prefer not to think about.

Such an approach is valuable in getting the attention and interest of a prospect who is not inclined to treat the sales propositions seriously, someone who refuses to become emotionally involved with the problem at hand. Amazingly, some people refuse to come to grips with critical problems; they seem to feel that problems they don't think about will go away. The shock treatment may get through this defense mechanism, thereby allowing the salesperson to get on with the presentation.

The Showmanship Approach

Certain situations call for unusual efforts if a prospect's attention and interest are to be obtained. There have been numerous shows put on for the benefit of some important prospect who appreciates imagination and showmanship. One young man seeking employment with an advertising agency was having great difficulty obtaining an interview with the top executive; so he had himself boxed up and delivered into the inner sanctum by an express company. Another sales rep took space on a large billboard on the route his prospect took to and from home. It declared, "Mr. B. Dunn: You are losing $300 every day you fail to see me! Signed: R. Davis, Sharp Tool Company." There is no limit to what an enterprising person can do to dramatize an approach when the situation warrants it.

The Question Approach

Asking questions to open an interview is an art. It can be used in conjunction with other approaches, particularly the consumer-benefit approach, or it can stand on its own. "What will you be doing in the year 2010?" just might grab a young man in such a way that he would talk about retirement planning. "Are you big enough to use automated production equipment profitably?" might cause the president of a growing manufacturing company to answer, "I don't know. How big have I got to be?" And then the two can get right to the heart of the matter.

Psychological questioning immediately gets the prospects attention, interest, and participation in the affair. It focuses the mind on an essential element in the proposition, which gets the presentation off to a good start.

A woman selling a collection service used an approach consisting of the simple question: "I'm not sure if you're the person I'm looking for. Have you 30 accounts on your books that you have given up as dead?"

Of course, the questions must be well framed. Too many salespeople fall into the slack habit of greeting their prospects with, "How's business?" The space buyer for a large advertising agency kept a record of what sales reps said to him when they first approached.

Out of the 14 so-called sales reps who called in one day, 12 opened the interview with "How's business?" "How do things look?" "Things picking up much yet?" The salesmanager of a large furniture company says that four out of five salespeople open their talks with "How's tricks?" or "How's business?"

Such an approach may suffice in prosperous times, but it is loaded with dynamite when business is not so good. And when did anyone ever find prospects enthusiastic about business? It is a part of the buyer's defense to pull a long face, to insist that he cannot afford to buy, to swear that the salesperson's product has been given a thorough trial and did not move or perform. To ask the buyer how business is invites only trouble.

Other approaches are equally ineffective. "Well, anything new since I saw you last?" "No, I guess not, Jane." And that's that.

"You haven't given me an order for four months. Isn't it about time you slipped me one?" Did this person get the order?

"I was just passing by and dropped in to see if you needed anything in our line today. Anything doing?" This approach is so weak and yet so widely used that it merits discussion. It is poor psychology to make the buyer think that the call is so casual. It makes it too easy to turn the salesperson down. It is much better to give the impression that the buyer's problem has been given the most thorough consideration and that this call is a very special one made for the purpose of presenting a very special recommendation.

"Mr. Prospect, I was thinking about you all last evening," Is Mr. Prospect likely to yell, "I'm not interested!"?

One industrial sales rep selling forklift trucks would open an interview with the question, "Would you like to save $6300 on your warehouse handling costs this next year?" What executive could say no to that question? The sales rep had, of course, determined the figure from a preapproach survey.

A representative for a manufacturer in the electronics field catches a purchasing agent's attention and interest by asking, "What one electronic item that you are now buying is giving you the biggest headaches?" He had found that most p.a.'s have many headaches for which they are seeking the right "aspirin." This opening allows the salesman to dwell on the problems that the prospect considers to be the most serious and about which he is most apt to do something. Sometimes he asks, "What electronic equipment you are now buying do you feel is most overpriced?" The point of this additional question is to find in what areas he would meet the least pressure on prices and could be most competitive.

This art of asking the right questions serves several purposes. It forces the prospect to talk in the areas chosen by you. It elicits information of tremendous value, thereby pushing the preapproach to satisfying depth. It focuses the prospect's attention on the problem they are most eager to solve, thus guiding the salesperson into the shortest path to a sale.

There are some basic principles you should observe in phrasing questions. First, the more specific the question, the better. Compare these questions: "Would you like to save several thousands of dollars in labor costs?" and "Would you like to save $15,500 next year on your costs of handling goods in process?" Which is most likely to whet the interest of the prospect and move smoothly into the sale of conveyor systems?

Second, whenever possible, the question should be tailored for the prospect's situation, based on data obtained through a good preappraoch.

Third, the question should be aimed at the major

consumer benefit in which the prospect will be interested. Aim at the major buying motives rather than the minor ones. If you are convinced that the prospect is most interested in saving money, then your question should be directed to that motive. If you feel that status is the most important motive, then your question should suggest that your product will help the prospect to gain status.

Fourth, there are some areas in which you should be extremely cautious about asking questions. There are some things that people will not talk about even when asked. Generally, people hesitate to talk of their financial condition to strangers. Before you can elicit such information you must establish your need to know the data for the good of the prospect as well as your ability to respect confidences. A rapport must be established, which may take some time. Sometimes you can probe these areas by using hypothetical data that you believe approximate the prospect's situation, thus allowing the buyer to keep his own exact data confidential.

Making the Presentation

Your presentation should arouse the prospect's desire to own your product or service. After he has decided he wants it, you can convince him that the deal is sound, that your product is good, and that his fears are groundless. But there is no use doing these things until you have established the need.

The objectives of your presentation are to make the prospect aware that he has a problem, and to prove that you and your firm are reliable.

Creating Believability

Your behavior can either enhance or detract from your believability. Seldom does a prospect separate you from the statements you make: you are judged from all the evidence at hand, which includes both your statements and your behavior.

Perhaps no one thing does more to build confidence than a display of genuine unselfishness on your part. If you really have the buyer's interest at heart you gain the buyer's confidence as you prove it by deeds.

The necktie rep says to the dealer: "Now here's a number that didn't sell so well in the test markets. Men just didn't like it. Guess their wives didn't either. Here's another that did a little better but not too well. "I wouldn't urge you to stock either one. But here's one that the customers really went for. I figure you could handle two dozen. That about right?"

You should be telling the truth. All that the dealer who gets bad goods will think about every time he sees them gathering dust on his shelves is: "That no-good peddler stuck me with those dogs!" Those who call regularly on retailers know that their long-run success depends on gaining the dealer's confidence. This is not likely to happen if you fail to deal fairly and truthfully.

THE REAL BASIS FOR BELIEVABILITY IS TRUTHFULNESS AND FAIR DEALING WITH THE PROSPECT OVER THE LONG HAUL

Industrial sales presentations are built around an extensive use of facts, case histories, demonstrations, and trial uses. The last technique should be stressed, for few things are more potent in selling than letting the prospective customer use the product. The inertia blocking the adoption of any new product is difficult to overcome. People just don't change their ways easily, and for good reason. They've seen all sorts of promising new products come along, which failed to deliver. Thus they are leery of the claims made for innovations.

Even so, many industrial buyers are reluctant to allow even a trial, for they are afraid of harming their production process in some manner if the new product fails to work as promised. It's not always easy to get a trial placement.

A substitute for a trial use is to install one unit somewhere and then bring the industrial buyer to see it. Bear in mind that at times there are millions of dollars in potential profits to be made if the product turns out to be everything that is being claimed for it. So take your industrial prospect to see the product in use and talk to the people using it.

The sales library in each Xerox sales office has a large number of case histories of applications of Xerox machines. A Xerox sales rep planning to call on a university librarian could go to the Xerox archives to locate a case history of a Xerox machine being used in the library at the University of Colorado, for example. After studying that particular application the rep could show it to the prospective buyer.

Specific versus Vague Statements

Accurate knowledge of your proposition enables you to make specific statements instead of vague, general ones.

Many statements sound specific when they are not. The sales rep for a small car might say, "This car will get 30 miles a gallon." This sounds specific, but it could be more specific. "Compared with a car that delivers 15 miles per gallon you save $33.33 every 1000 miles if you pay $1.00 a gallon. If you drive 10,000 miles a year, that is $333. You can buy quite a bit with $333 even these days."

Incidentally, two important words in sales rep's vocabulary are "for instance." Use them because they promise something specific. One should avoid the use of such general words as "economical," "automatic," "efficient," "modern," or "attractive." One should try to define each of such words in specific terms. "Economical" becomes $3.20 per month saved."

Early Claims Should Be Conservative

Besides one's overall behavior, there are some definite things that can be done to gain the prospect's confidence.

Strong claims should not be made early in the interview, for they are likely to be discounted by the buyer. However, if early claims are conservative and creditable, the subsequent ones may be bolder.

Some professional buyers deliberately lie in wait to pounce on the first exaggerated statement made by a salesperson by demanding proof of it then and there. They seize the offensive and never let the poor sales rep recover his poise.

Indeed, it does not pay, in the long run, to exaggerate at any stage of the interview, especially if you are trying to build up a reputation and a clientele. Don't promise more than you can deliver, but deliver what you have promised. If "a satisfied customer is the best advertisement," then a dissatisfied customer is a firm's worst advertisement and is more likely to talk than is the satisfied one because of wanting to get even.

Tests as Confidence Winners

Another method of winning the buyer's confidence is through tests of various sorts, "Just taste that. Did you ever taste anything so good?" the enthusiastic salesman for grape juice exclaims while giving the prospect a taste of the product, kept cold in a thermos bottle. The clothing or textile saleswoman submits her product to the well-known tests. The paper salesman has his customer tear his product, hold it to the light at certain angles, and test it in other ways.

The headline on an article in *Sales Management* proclaims: "If you sell to the industrial market, get 'em to test it . . . and it's nine-tenths sold."

The willingness with which one submits the product to these tests is a factor in gaining the prospect's confidence. If you are eager to have your product thoroughly tested, the prospect is impressed by your attitude.

Some tests, although impressive to the unskilled prospect, are unconvincing to the expert buyer. The sales-person will do well to develop the preapproach in such a way as to avoid the mistake of using a "grandstand" type of test on a buyer who knows it lacks value. With an experienced buyer it may be best to permit the buyer to conduct his own tests.

The Guarantee

This is a powerful sales aid, particularly in selling a new product or selling to a new prospect. Of course, the guarantee is of value only insofar as the company issuing it is reliable, but even with this qualification or guarantee makes it easier to win the confidence of buyers.

Guarantees are of varying strength; some are absolute, like those used by the big mail-order houses, while others cover only certain matters such as material and workmanship. New products will often sell more readily if they are warranted, but established products of good quality find less need for such support.

Show Records

A women's ready-to-wear rep proved to a small-town merchant that the firm's line was really moving by showing bona fide reorders placed by merchants known to the buyer.

An industrial machine salesman wanted to convince the prospect that his turret lathe required minimal repair. He produced records for a sample of installations showing each repair call the firm had received from the customers.

Plant Tours

An electronics firm was attempting to convince a large prime contractor that its quality-control system would ensure the maintenance of output quality so that it could be placed on the approved list of suppliers. Several executives of the prime contractor were flown out to the plant to inspect firsthand the facilities and quality-control methods in operation. They were convinced.

Many food manufacturers have always encouraged tours of their plants to convince the public of the cleanliness of their operations. Such tours can communicate many messages to the public and prospects. Meeting and talking with the seller's personnel may increase the confidence the buyer has in the firm.

Talking with Customers

This is akin to reading testimonials, yet it may be more effective. Many a sales rep has saved a sale by suggesting to a prospect, "Just pick up your phone and call So-and-So and ask her about it. I'll pay the charge."

Sometimes one is at a loss as to precisely which method to use in gaining the prospect's complete confidence. To save time you may say: "I know that I make statements that may sound almost too good to be true. If you have any doubt about something I have said, what would convince you of its truth?"

The prospect may be thinking of a free trial or some particular test or demonstration, and will tell you so. If you can go along with the suggestion, you may make the sale right there.

Other Basic Strategies of the Presentation

Although you must devise many specific strategies and tactics for selling your particular line of products, some general strategies are applicable to most goods.

Selling Should Not Be a Battle

"Keep arguments out of the selling talk" is one of the best pieces of advice given to young salespeople by their managers. One famous salesman, Rube Wardell, used to say, "Sure, you can prove to the buyer and to anybody that's around him that he doesn't know what he is talking about. But what does that get you? There's no nourishment in showing the buyer up. He isn't going to thank you for it. More often than not he'll remember the incident, and sooner or later it will cost you business."

Some salespeople seem to go out of their way to arouse the antagonism of the buyer. One of the commonest forms of this reverse technique is to make a remark to this effect: "Well, sooner or later you are going to buy from me. I'll be seeing you."

Keep the Interview Friendly

Buyers are not computer-like mechanisms who arrive at a decision by feeding facts into their brains and turning out the right answers. They are human beings and prefer to do business with people they like. If they like a certain salesperson they will give that person longer interviews, will listen more sympathetically to the story, and are more likely to give the person repeat business. While it is not good policy to buy from someone just because of friendship, if other factors are equal the friend will usually get the business—and should.

Bear in mind that the buyer is often glad to stop a few minutes and talk with a friendly soul. He may have been having one of those days when everything goes wrong, when he is forced to make unpleasant decisions, when he is having arguments with too many people. His nerves are on edge, his blood pressure is up, and he wishes he could quit and raise chickens. Then a smiling sales rep is ushered in, bringing a new idea that promises to help solve some problem confronting the harassed buyer. He brings a breath of the outside world, together with some trade gossip and always helpful ideas. They buyer may act tense and scowl firecely at first, but this may be a holdover from hectic hours just preceding. The buyer who feels you are really friendly relaxes for a few minutes and is glad of the chance to do so.

We have said many times that a sales interview should never be an argument. Rather, it should take on the aspect of a friendly conversation on a topic of mutual interest. With a friend we do not quibble over some minor point; we feel an urge to agree. The interview moves smoothly.

If the buyer is already a customer, one must work hard at the job of retaining the friendship. Watch out for that customer's interests in every way, such as pushing for prompt deliveries, careful packing, or selling aids that have been promised. One must be dependable— absolutely.

A buyer related to the author an incident that had stuck in his memory for 20 years. He had placed an initial order with a certain salesman who had promised delivery on January 15, since the stuff was needed by January 16. At four o'clock in the afternoon of January

15, the buyer's telephone rang. It was the salesman who had promised to make delivery that day. "I'm driving a company truck with your stuff in it and I'll get to your place by 8 o'clock tonight. We ran into a lot of unavoidable delays, and the roads are slippery, but we'll beat that deadline. Will someone be there to take the stuff inside at 8 o'clock?" That buyer, after 20 years, feelingly commented, "That salesman kept my business as long as he called on me. And he never let me down in any way."

Timing

There are wrong times to try to make a sale. Prospects can be so busy or preoccupied with other problems that there is no room for the proposition in their thinking. Someone whose plant has just burned down is in no mental state to listen to anything unless it is something that will directly alleviate the immediate problems.

Prospects can be in unfavorable mental or emotional states when it is difficult to communicate with them in a rational manner. A man who has just had a death in the family is not in the mood to listen to someone extolling the virtues of a turret lathe.

The financial abilities of prospects vary with the times. The person who has just heard his accountant report a large increase in profits is a different buyer from the one who has been told that he suffered a loss last quarter.

Obviously, one should take the timing factor into consideration if some significant event is discovered during the preapproach, and one must be prepared to bow out quickly and gracefully upon encountering some unexpected event that places the prospect in an unfavorable frame of mind.

A Good Listener May Sell Too

Many a salespeople seem to feel that it is necessary to keep up a constant flow of talk, that the enemy must be pinned down by a ceaseless chatter of oral machine guns.

More experienced reps have learned that it is wise to let the prospect do quite a bit of talking, especially if the person appears favorably inclined toward the proposition. If the prospect wishes to elaborate on some advantage of the product, it is good strategy to keep silent and let the buyer sell himself.

Indeed, many skilled persuaders make a practice of presenting their claims in a rather sketchy style, allowing their prospects to fill in the gaps and arrive at their own conclusions. Under such circumstances the prospect is likely to exclaim, "Then this would be true, too, wouldn't it?" This is precisely what the salesperson is striving for - to help the buyer reach his own conclusions. When these tactics are employed, the buyer feels smugly pleased because he has been able to figure the thing out more or less independently and forthwith embraces and champions the new idea as his own. Thus the prospect sells himself the proposition.

Obviously, one can use these methods only when the prospect is not firmly opposed and has sufficient mental agility to leap the gaps in the presentation and research the desired conclusions without being led step by step.

In selling the opinionated buyer, one may fare better by not talking much. Also, when two people are shopping together they may wish to discuss the articles without interference from the salesperson and are likely to appreciate being allowed to make their own decisions. As long as they are interested in the article and are talking it over, one can afford to await the time when it may be necessary to put in a word to save the sale. If this does not prove necessary, all is well. Many buyers prefer to be allowed to consider a proposition carefully without being pushed.

If one insists on doing too much of the talking, several things are likely to happen.

The prospect loses interest. He can keep his mind moving better if he is moving physically. It is always the students in the lecture who go to sleep - never the professor. A prospect who is allowed to talk a share of the time will be more likely to grasp quickly what is said.

The prospect is mulling over in his mind the things that he would like to say, instead of giving attention to the things that the sales rep is saying. This is fatal to successful selling.

The longer the prospect is forced to bottle up his questions and objections, the more inflated they become. Permitting the prospect to do his share of the talking often discloses the obstacles to his buying; it brings out objections; it airs his opinions on the proposition. With this knowledge the sale can be more intelligently planned.

Another advantage of letting the prospect talk is that it makes him feel that he is not being high-pressured. It gives him the impression that the sales rep is trying to learn all about his problems so that he can render him a real service. It builds confidence. It relaxes tensions.

How can we give the impression that we are really listening?

We should listen with our eyes; we should look directly at the speaker.

We should permit or even encourage our facial expressions to respond to the statements of the speaker.

Smile, compress lips, raise eyebrows, nod head, or appear to reflect a moment on some point.

We may occasionally comment on a statement made by the speaker, such as "So that's why they use aluminum in that part." "Yours is a larger outfit than I realized." This shows that we are listening. We may even use a rising inflection, in our voices indicating a question on some point.

We should be careful not to interrupt with some "offbeat" comment or remark, thereby revealing that we are not in step.

By listening - really listening - we accomplish several desirable objectives:

> We are complimenting the prospect and building up his ego.
>
> We are impressing him with our intelligence and interest
>
> We are learning something. It has been truly said that nobody learns much while talking. But while our prospect is talking, we are learning things.
>
> We are making him like us and are putting him in a mood to be helpful to us.

This discussion should not be interpreted as meaning that the sales rep should do little talking at the opening of the interview. It is usually necessary to talk long enough to get the interview well under way and to prevent being turned down before having a chance to present the proposition. Once the interview is assured, it is time to let the prospect take part in it.

Notice that one does not lose control over the situation by allowing the prospect to talk: the sale is going as planned. One can maintain dominance even while listening.

The Setting for the Presentation

Sometimes the smallest details can influence the outcome of a sale. Certainly the immediate environment in which the presentation is to take place can most definitely affect the sale. For that reason, some forethought should be given to where one wants to make the presentation. Often it is wise to avoid making sales presentations in the prospect's place of business—confusion and interruptions can be ruinous to the train of thought required for the transaction. Pick a place where both you and the prospect can meet in comfort and in privacy. Frequently a prospect's behavior becomes more sociable when not in a business setting.

As you enter the presence of the buyer, try to size up the situation, and plan quickly how to arrange things to your advantage.

Some buyers try to make the salesperson tell his story while they are standing in the outer office or in the doorway. The salesperson should request a better chance to make the presentation, perhaps basing this on the need for a place to show samples, set up a projection machine, and so on.

Once inside the buyer's office, quickly appraise certain factors. Consider lighting, for example, since you wish to show your samples or photographs in the most favorable light.

Noise is likely to interfere with the interview, unless it is noise to which the buyer has become so accustomed that he scarcely notices it. If it can be eliminated by closing a door or a window, perhaps this should be done. Regular noises of a factory, for instance, cannot be entirely excluded although they may be minimized.

Sometimes it is necessary to shift the scene of the interview to a quieter spot, but this possibility should be anticipated rather than left to the last minute.

The very fact that you are forced to raise your voice to be heard above some distracting noise reduces effectiveness. The interview loses its relaxed conversational tone, which is bad. Too, the voice usually becomes more strident and unpleasant under these conditions, which may jar on the sensibilities of the prospect and cause him to cut short the interview. Noise can ruin a sales presentation.

Handling Competition

Few sales are made without encountering competition of some sort. You must be prepared to handle it to avoid giving the prospect the idea that you can't. Certainly the prospect is aware of some competitive offers in most instances, but it is surprising how often a salesperson will encounter a prospect who is unaware of some of the leading competitors in the field. Hence wise salespeople are reluctant to bring up the matter of competition for fear that they will be telling the prospect something he does not know.

A business executive was shopping for an inexpensive car for his son as a high school graduation present. He had been attracted to Saab by some advertising, so he dropped by a Saab dealership for a demonstration. Throughout the presentation the Saab salesman was preoccupied with relating how his product was superior to the Fiat and VW. It seemed to the prospect that in this salesman's mind the other two cars were serious competition; so the prospect decided that he had better check them out for himself even though he had been

unaware of them previously. He ended up buying a
Fiat. Let sleeping dogs . . . !

Praise and Pass On

Of the three views on the handling of competition,
the first holds that salespeople should not mention their
competitors except in praise. When and if the prospect
brings up the matter of competition, praise it and pass
on. "Yes, that is a good product. But ours is better! . . . "
By ignoring competition entirely, the prospect is not led
to consider the other fellow's proposition. The motto of
the group seems to be, "Sell your own goods, and let
the other guys sell theirs."

Unfortunately, this may not always be the best strategy. A competitive brand may loom large in the prospect's mind and ignoring it will do little to dislodge its
place in the picture. In fact, some prospects will not
bring up another product that is their favorite for fear
that the sales rep will show them the folly of their
thinking. There is security in silence. If the sales rep is
to handle that competition, it is first necessary to get
the prospect to bring it out and talk about it. Smart car
salespeople determine the competitive setting early in
a sale. They ask what other cars the prospects have seen
and which they like best. "Of all the cars you have seen
so far, which one do you like best?" The answer to this
question provides a great deal of information to the
perceptive sales rep. If the prospect answers, "The
Trans-Am!" then it would be folly to try to push a four-
door sedate sedan at him. Most car sales reps dread
attempting a sale to prospects who have only begun to
shop for cars because they know that no matter how
good a deal is offered to such prospects, they will still
feel it necessary to look around. The wise car salesper-

son prefers to get prospects after they have seen the other brands; then there is hope of closing a sale.

Meet It Head On

The second view is that competition must be met, that it cannot be ignored. Indeed, some advocates of the theory want a return to the day when competitors were not afraid to point out the weaknesses of the other's products. These stern old warriors feel that business has perhaps become too effete.

A sales rep of men's work clothes is trying to sell to a dealer. The sales rep's line has a new serged seam instead of the felled type. The dealer brings out from his stock a garment with felled seam and demands, "What's the matter with this seam?"

Sales rep: "There's nothing the matter with it. The Army uses it. It wears as well as any seam you can put on a garment. But I can give you two reasons why we have quit using the felled seams. It doesn't lie as neatly as our serged seam, and it can't be repaired on an ordinary sewing machine. Our serged seam can be. Now, since this new seam wears just as well as the felled seam, looks better, and is more easily repaired, we feel sure it's going to sell more work clothes for you."

This is a far cry from the bitter, ranting knocking of competition indulged in by some salespeople. "You'd be nuts to buy that junk. Won't stand up. Repair bills every month. Hard to get quick service on it, too."

When it seems necessary to make a comparison between your product and a competitor's, avoid going into detail and trying to cover every point. Rather, cover only those features that seem to interest your prospect the most. Four or five of these are usually sufficient. If your car prospect has dwelt on rear-end drag (he had a steep driveway), give him the figures on this point. If he tours a good deal, go into details on trunk room, air-conditioning, gasoline consumption, reasons for easy riding. To cover every comparative advantage is to confuse him and kill his interest.

This involves knowing where your product is strong and your competitor's is weak. Better stick to these, if you can.

Some people believe that it is shrewd to implant in the mind of a prospect a seed of doubt concerning a competing product. They may do this adroitly by telling something they have heard about it; or they may come out more frankly with their own opinion. If the sales-person and prospect are well acquainted with each other, the salesperson may be more frank than if they were strangers. But a seed of doubt, thus planted, may grow into a big doubt—big enough to prevent the purchase of the competing product.

However, this adverse comment by the sales rep must have a basis in fact. Frequently the prospect may ask the competitor about this point and may receive such a convincing reply that his faith in the first sales rep is shattered. But, if the reply is not convincing, the first sales rep may gain the prospect's confidence and make the sale.

Recognize, but Handle with Care

A third view lies somewhere between the extremes. It is doubtless wise to avoid vigorous "knocking" of competitors, and yet it seems impossible to ignore them completely. Knocking competitors creates the impression that the seller is finding competition to be keen, is feeling it strongly. The inference is that he feels so antagonistic toward the other fellow largely because he has suffered much at his hands. The next step in the prospect's reasoning is, "If this fellow loses so much business to his competitor, probably the competitor has a good proposition. I ought to look into it."

Another result of too vigorous criticism of competitors is to destroy confidence in the proposition in general. Back in the days when life insurance was newer, two rival solicitors in a small Illinois town agreed to a debate in the local "opera house." They had been so bitter in their denunciations of each other that the debate attracted a large crowd. The debators devoted almost their entire time to pointing out the weaknesses, crookedness, and general evils of the opposing insurance companies. They provided much entertainment for the citizenry; but when the debate was over, nobody in town dared to buy insurance from either company.

The principle also applies to retail selling when salespeople attack the reliability of their competitors. A young man lived in a small town that supported only two jewelry stores. He wanted to buy a diamond ring—the diamond ring. The demand was actively present. Each dealer cast so many aspersions upon the integrity of his competitor that the young man concluded that, since he knew very little about diamonds and could easily be deceived as to the stone's real value, he would do better to patronize neither of the local dealers but go to a jeweler in a neighboring city.

A purchasing agent relates an incident of a salesman's knocking a competitor which illustrates the disastrous result (to the salesman):

"I was in the market for a supply of shipping cases. Bids were received, including one from a firm with which I had done considerable business and one from another company with which I had less an acquaintance but which bore a fine reputation. A salesman from the first firm put in his appearance and asked me what concerns were bidding. I told him, although I refrained from mentioning prices. Immediately he started in, 'Well, of course, you know Jim is a good fellow, but can he deliver the goods as you want them? His factory is small, and I am not too sure of his methods. Can he give you what you want? You know he has not had much experience with your product.' And so on."

Good natured knocking in a way, but knocking nevertheless. What was the result? I was filled with curiosity to see the inside of Jim's factory and to talk it over with him, so I made an inspection tour. He got the order and, incidentally, did a good job. There was a simple case of a man selling his competitor's goods, for it was really his discouraging comments that created in me a curiosity to go and see for myself, with an outcome extremely disappointing to the knocker.

The Deadly Comparison

Some manufacturers of mechanical products train their sales reps to make a point-by-point comparison between their product and the one competing product that stands highest in the prospect's opinion. They do this on paper, too, putting down each point and checking, in one of the two columns, which of the two products is superior on that point. When the process is finished, it is expected that the sales rep's product will have more check marks in its column than the competing product does. This is bare-fisted selling, but it is sometimes necessary and effective, especially if the comparisons are made in a fair and objective manner.

A variation of this method is to take a sheet of paper and draw a line down the middle, making two columns. Put the name of the competing product at the top of one column and your product and the top of the other. Then put the price of each—say, $220 and $250—in the proper column. The competing product is cheaper, so the sales rep's task is to justify her higher price. She therefore mentions one exclusive feature of her product and says; "Would you say that this feature would be worth $1 a year to you? That's a very conservative estimate, isn't it? All right, this will last much longer than 10 years, but let's be conservative again and say it will last 10 years. That's $10 benefit you get from this feature." Thus the saleswoman proceeds feature by feature until she has built up value exceeding the $30 difference in price.

In cases where the prospect has already bought from a competitor, the salesman must exercise care in making comments on the competitor's proposition, for to criticize it is to question the taste or judgment of the buyer. Tact must be used, as the sales rep for office filing equipment realized when she tried to persuade a prospect to change his system completely and install a new one costing nearly $2000. She did not make the prospect feel that he had shown a lack of acumen in installing the first system; rather, she complimented him on it but showed tactfully how enlarged business, changed conditions, and new inventions in the way of equipment now made a change desirable.

Competitive Intelligence
Another reason for paying attention to competitors is pointed out by a manufacturer: "I don't believe in competitive salesmanship with the trade, but I am convinced that it is the greatest mistake in the world to dodge discussing competition with my own salesmen. I used to 'tend to my own knitting' so hard that I didn't know half that was going on in the field. Now I ask all my salesmen to send as quickly as possible any new competitive products that appear in their territories.

"This mere willingness to look into the other fel-

low's goods has a tonic effect on our men. It shows at
least that I don't propose to be caught napping: and if
there's anything that discourages salesmen, it's having
competing articles constantly discussed by the trade
while 'the house goes on sleeping.'

"We believe thoroughly in letting all the facts come
out. A salesman on the road is constantly hearing about
the other fellow's good points and his own weak ones.
That is why a salesman should be brought back to the
home office at frequent intervals and resold from top to
bottom on his line. Then he will not be tempted to use
defensive, competitive salesmanship."

One IBM typewriter saleswoman was placed in a
most embarrassing position when a customer called her
to cancel an order he had previously given for a new
IBM electronic typewriter because he had found one
that met his needs far better—the Adler SC2000. The
IBM saleswoman said that she had a machine that had
everything the Adler had to offer and more. She asked
to see the buyer the next morning, which was arranged.
Unfortunately it quickly became apparent to both the
buyer and the saleswoman that not only did IBM not
have a competitive model but that she was unaware of
the Adler machine.

You cannot meet the competition unless you know
all about it.

With a bit of experience sales trainees quickly learn
which competitive products pose the most potent threat
and are made aware of their own products competitive
strengths and weaknesses. Thus it is possible to anticipate and forestall competitive arguments during the
presentation. If you know that your product is relatively
high priced, you will continually be building up the
product's value—higher quality, additional features—
during the interview. You can meet the claims you know

will be made—meet them with talking points showing the superiority of your product in those very particulars or in offsetting advantages. In this way you can shrink competitive advantages or claims in the mind of the prospect before they are brought out into the open. This can be done without mentioning the competitor by name, thereby avoiding an argument or engaging in a rough knocking session.

It goes without saying that a thorough knowledge of competing propositions must underlie any effort to eliminate them. This knowledge should include such matters as trend of sales, how current models are catching on, service given, delivery performance, value of their dealer assistance, advertising and sales promotion program, various trade practices, their real price. It is helpful to know just where your competition is most vulnerable. Talk with owners of competing products.

Be familiar with the claims made by your competitors. Watch their advertising; get hold of their sales literature; visit their salesrooms or showrooms. Ask your good customers what they hear about competitors.

Learn what your competitors are saying about your product. Get competitors to try to sell you, if possible. Make a list of their claims against your product, line, or company.

Finally, it will help if you can identify just where your chief competition lies in each particular sale. Then you can slant your demonstration accordingly.

It is hard to remain silent in the face of unfair competition. Indeed, it may be a sound idea to fight back vigorously at a competitor who is using unethical means to ruin you. This is just about the only time it is wise to mention a competitor by name, and even here it is usually better to wait until the prospect has brought this competitor into the conversation.

If your prospect has a good friend who is in competition with you for the prospect's business, it does not pay to criticize that friend. Rather, it is wise to present your own proposition so effectively that the prospect's self-interest overcomes the desire to buy from the friend. If the question is raised, you can point out briefly and simply that, if the competitor is actually a true friend of the prospect, the competitor would want the prospect to buy the product that would best serve the prospect's purposes. Sometimes the alleged friendship may not be so warm as you imagine it to be; perhaps the prospect is eager to end the arrangement, since the "friend" may be selling on friendship alone and not providing the best service or the best product. It is by no means a hopeless situation to be selling against a friend of the prospect.

Negative salesmanship usually avails nothing. Suppose a sales rep for a fruit commission house walks into the prospect's place of business, hands him a wormy, gnarled apple with the remark that this is the kind of apple his competitor is selling, and then turns around and walks out. Such a salesperson would be adjudged mentally incompetent. The negative idea regarding competitor's goods should be merely supplementary to the positive idea concerning the sales rep's product if a sale is to result.

An attitude of absolute fairness toward competitors, even when it is necessary to speak disparagingly of their goods, should be preserved. One should say nothing derogatory that cannot be substantiated at once, and one should be careful about saying even that if it does not seem necessary.

One reason for keeping on as friendly terms as possible with competitors is that the mean things said about them always get back to them and cause them to be even more vigorous and active in their efforts to win business. If your adverse comments are not true, competitors may adopt retaliatory measures.

Salespeople will, therefore, do well to avoid mentioning their competitors; unavoidable comparisons should be made in a spirit of fairness, and no statements should be made that cannot at once be substantiated. The ethics of business are improving, and salespeople should help to lead the way.

About Objections

Objections are an integral part of the sales process. Once you accept the idea that objections are to be expected and are normal, you will have a better philosophical attitude with which to approach them.

How should you regard objections? If you are a beginner, you may feel disheartened when an objection is raised. It may appear as a refusal to buy. Sometimes it is, although it need not be. After all, you know the person is a good prospect because you preapproach qualified the firm as such. You know your product meets its needs and that it can afford the product. So why fear an objection?

Veteran salespeople welcome the expressed objection, for they know that it is a sales aid rather than a hindrance. One of the most difficult prospects to sell is the "clam who does not show any interest in the proposition, who does not comment on it at all, who merely sits in stony silence while the sales rep strives to pierce this armor of indifference. The salesperson who is trying to sell to such "clams" cannot tell whether she is making a favorable or an unfavorable impression and wishes fervently that the prospect would give some clue to how the sale is progressing and what the prospect is thinking about.

The prospect who voices honest objections is assisting you by disclosing how far away you are from a sale. The prospect is also providing more valuable information about what it will take to make the sale than all of your preapproach data.

Sometimes the prospect remains unconvinced simply because you have failed to answer some question. When that point is cleared up, the prospect may be ready to buy. A prospect being shown a forklift truck fears that it may be too small to handle the loads in his warehouse, otherwise he likes it. A demonstration that the truck can handle the job may get the order immediately.

A veteran sales rep commented that he always looks upon an objection as a request for information. "Objections arise," he declared, "for one of two reasons. Either the prospect does not understand what I have told him, or he does not grasp the significance of my point. So I consider objections as requests for more facts and respond by giving the information desired." "I'm glad you brought that up," is an excellent way for a sales rep to make the prospect feel that his objections are welcomed. "That is a good question, and I am glad to give you full information about it." is the way many salespersons handle objections. Never indicate you fear any objection, but don't reply in the same way to every objection. It soon becomes monotonous and phony. Use variations in language and methods.

Avoid Arguments in Handling Objections

This is not the first time that the importance of avoiding arguments has been mentioned. However, there is probably a greater tendency to argue when answering objections than in other parts of the sale. It is so easy to do and so disastrous. You can suddenly realize you have slipped into an argument with the prospect, yet not know how you got there. No matter how violently your prospect disagrees—or how directly he contradicts, or how persistently he tries to argue—don't argue with him.

The oft-quoted experience of Benjamin Franklin on this subject serves to stress the value of the proper attitude: "A Quaker friend informed me I was not content with being in the right when discussing any point but had to be overbearing and insolent about it—of which he convinced me by mentioning several instances. Endeavoring to cure myself of this fault, which I now realized had lost me many an argument, I made the following rule: to forbear all direct contradictions of the sentiments of others and all overpositive assertions of my own.

"Thereafter, when another asserted something I thought an error, I denied myself the pleasure of contradicting him abruptly and of showing immediately some absurdity in his proposition. Instead, I began by observing that . . . in certain cases or circumstances his opinion would be right . . . but in the present case there appeared or seemed to me some difference, etc.

"I soon found the advantage of this change in my manner. The conversations I engaged in went on more pleasantly. The modest way in which I proposed my opinions procured them a readier reception and less contradiction. I had less mortification when I was found to be in the wrong, and I more easily prevailed upon others to give up their mistakes and join with me when I happened to be right."

This Franklin philosophy is echoed by a present-day paint manufacturer which advices its salespeople to "use antiargument phrases" in handling questions and objections. Example: "Don't say, 'This paint has the best reputation in town.' Do say, 'From what others tell me, I'm led to believe that this paint has the best reputation in town.' " When the prospect objects, "Your price is too high," the salesperson is instructed to reply, "I don't blame you. Many others have thought the price was too high until they found out what this paint would do for them." Instead of flatly stating, "This paint will save you a lot of money." these salespeople are taught to say, "I don't blame you if you doubt what I am going to say, but this will save you a lot of money." These are sample "antiargument phrases."

Many salespeople listen intently to a prospect's objection and try to find some point in it with which they can agree. They restate this point of agreement and then proceed from there.

Avoid Irrelevant Objections
Too often salespeople permit themselves to be led into a controversy on a point unrelated to the proposition that they are selling. If the buyer is prejudiced, if he holds odd ideas, it is not your business to convert him on those irrelevant points. You are interested solely in the buyer's opinion of your proposition and should not concern yourself with his views on anything else.

Of particular importance are the matters of politics, religion, local issues, controversial persons in the news, and other "hot" topics. Usually little can be gained and everything can be lost if you allow yourself to be drawn into such discussions. Even if the two individuals are of the same party, they can easily fall into disagreement on minor issues and each leave the interview wondering about the other's basic intelligence. Unless the objection directly deals with the proposition at hand, the salesperson is wise not to take issue with the prospect's statement. If the prospect says that the world is flat, agree that a good deal of it surely looks like it and go on with your presentation. One office machines saleswoman lost a sale by getting into a discussion with the prospect over the appearance of the seller's new quarters. The prospect stated that he did not like the looks of the firm's new building. The saleswoman flew to her firm's defense, and the fat was in the fire. How silly!

Remove Objections Inoffensively

The essence of the Franklin theory is that the seller must learn to remove the objection or the "objectionable idea" from the mind of the prospect without giving offense. That is not always an easy thing to accomplish, depending on the tenacity with which the person clings to the objection raised. However, there are a number of ways to do it.

Exoneration from blame. You can exonerate the prospect from blame for expressing an objectionable idea. You can give such excuses as "I see that I did not clearly explain that feature." Or "I'm sorry that I misled you into thinking that . . . ." Or "It is quite easy to get that idea because of the complexity. . . . " Allow the prospect to save face and to minimize ego involvement when you say, in essence, that he is wrong.

Concessions. You can take the sting from a rebuttal by making some concessions before giving an answer. You might allow, "There is a great deal of truth in what you say, however . . . " Or "You know, I think you have a good thought there. That's a new point. I wonder if. . . . " People like to be told that their thoughts are great and they are not apt to be as resentful when you subsequently point out how their thoughts just aren't quite appropriate in this instance.

Deliberate attitude. Few people like their thoughts dealt with lightly; they want their ideas taken seriously and not passed off without due consideration. So the wise seller will say at such times, "You know, I'd like to mull that over a minute." Or "That's worth thinking about."

Others who agree. Somewhat in the same vein, the salesperson may be able to point out that there are many other people who agree with him; he is not alone in his idea. "You know, a great number of people believe that, however..." Or "Under similar circumstances, many people take your view, however..." are statements typical of handling objections by this means.

Paying tribute. At times you can pay tribute to the prospect in several ways, thereby erecting a buffer to protect the prospect's ego when the rebuttal is made. You may note that the prospect's motives are worthy by saying, "I admire your idealism and know that you are sincere, but...." Or "I know that you are honest and fair-minded, so allow me to show you just where our discussion went astray." At other times you can tell her that she is generally right by saying, "I know that you are an authority on this and are seldom wrong, however...." Or "I seldom hesitate in taking your advice, but...."

When Should an Objection Be Answered?

Most authorities agree that an objection should usually be met the moment it is raised. Several logical reasons support this policy.

Assume that the prospect raises an objection that the salesperson promises to answer. Not wishing to forget the objection and thinking that the salesperson may neglect to come back to it, the prospect concentrates on the point and is so preoccupied with it that he does not hear what the sales rep tells him in the meantime.

The prospect may get the impression that the salesperson does not have a valid answer and hopes the prospect may forget the objection if it is passed by for the moment. Confidence is shaken if the salesperson replies, "I'm glad you brought that up. I will come to it in just a few minutes."

The deferment of the answer also makes the prospect feel that you are just speaking your piece and are unable to reply to an objection without throwing yourself off stride.

When an early objection has been met effectively, it may turn out to have been the only obstacle to the order. Many salespeople seize upon an early well-met objection as a good closing time.

However, certain situations seem to justify postponing the answer. The situation of the early price objection frequently comes up in an interview before you have been able to buildup the product's value. It is often used by prospects as a stall to avoid listening to the proposition at all. When the objection is raised early in the interview, it may be postponed until the prospect has enough information about the proposition to be able to decide intelligently.

The saleswoman of air-conditioning equipment for the private house defers the premature question about price in this manner: "I can't give you the price until I've made a detailed study of how best to make your home comfortable in hot, muggy weather. There are many ways we can do it, but they vary greatly in price, so it takes some work to figure out how to do it for you for the lowest cost." Note how the saleswoman had turned the question into an opportunity to make a sales point. Also note how the saleswoman uses the words "home," "comfortable," "lowest cost," "hot," and "muggy" to stimulate the emotional reactions she wants in the prospect's mind.

The situation permitting postponement of the reply

arises when the objection concerns a subject different from the one being discussed but to be covered shortly.

Admittedly, from a purely psychological point of view, it would be advantageous to answer the prospect's question immediately, thus removing it from his mind. However, to do so often disrupts the point that you are trying to make and perhaps sidetracks the presentation into fruitless channels, thus bogging matters down.

Suppose a men's apparel representative is in the midst of presenting a fall line of sport coats when the dealer asks, "When am I going to get delivery on that last fill-in order I sent you last month?" Yes, prospects do throw in such nonsequiturs, much to the sales rep's dismay, but they can be handled. "I'll go get my invoice book to see after we finish working this line." It is important that the delaying answer be logical and reasonable, lest the prospect be irritated by nonsensical replies.

The situation calling for postponement of the answer to an objection arises when the question is trivial. In such a case, you may answer: "I appreciate your interest in this proposition, and I certainly want to answer all your questions, but it has been my experience that most of them will have been covered when we are through with the presentation. I am sure we could save time (and I know you are busy) if you will wait a few minutes and then ask your questions about anything that I have not covered." Most prospects are fair-minded enough to go along with such a suggestion if it is offered with a smile.

Forestalling Objections

Many objections can be forestalled. You will note that the same objections are raised in most cases at about the same place in the sale. A knowledge of the prospect helps in anticipating when certain common objections will come up.

Just what is meant by "forestalling" objections? It does not mean first stating the objection and then answering it. No mention of the objection is made, but the counterargument is presented in such a manner as to forestall the raising of the objection.

Salespeople for a machine costing several hundred dollars are taught to forestall the price objection. They know that most prospects will insist that they cannot afford it, so early in the interview the sales rep says, "I've talked with a number of people who apparently know you pretty well, and they all tell me that you are a first-class business executive—a real money-maker. I can see plenty of signs that you are doing well. I wouldn't have called on you unless I had assured myself of this. You aren't exactly facing bankruptcy, are you?" (With a broad smile.) In many cases the buyer will grin in return and admit that he is managing to stay in business. This forestalls the objection, "I can't afford it."

Other objections may be similarly forestalled. For example, many buyers want to "think it over."

The hard-selling salesperson may forestall this by saying: "I know you are a busy person, and I'm not going to waste your time. If I explain how my proposition will make you money and if I prove every point to your satisfaction will you tell me today how it strikes you and not ask me to come back next week? That's a fair proposal, isn't it?" After this it is difficult for the buyer to say he wants to think it over.

One securities salesman constantly encountered the two objections, I haven't got any money and I've got to talk it over with my wife (husband). He whipped these obstacles by opening the interview with the question,

"I am interested in talking with a person who has at least $3000 to put into a sound business venture and who makes decisions without having to consult a spouse. Are you such a person?" Once the prospect admitted to being qualified, he or she could hardly use those excuses as objections later.

When the sales rep has a particularly forceful answer to some common objection, it may be good strategy not to try to forestall it but to let the prospect raise it, so it can be used as the basis for a "trap close" in which the sales rep responds in effect to the prospect's objection, "If I answer your objection, will you buy?" Naturally, few salespeople would use those words, but they would try to get the prospect committed to buying upon meeting the objection.

Determining Hidden Objections

Up to this point we have assumed that if the prospect has an objection she states it, but it is not that simple. Prospects often hide their objections. To make the problem even more baffling, a prospect may offer a false objection, thereby wasting your time.

A common example are the prospects who cannot afford to pay the price asked. They are embarrassed to confess their poverty, so they give some other reason for not buying. Sometimes a prospect is too kind to come right out and say he thinks your product is junk. Or the prospects may simply say nothing at all, thus effectively concealing all their reactions.

The Stall

The stalling prospect offers some false objection that only obscures the real one. Let us first examine the stalling objection that is raised even before the sales-person has had a chance to present the proposition.

Suppose that a life insurance agent calls on Mr. Prospect to explain a new type of annuity policy. He is given a cordial welcome. For several minutes the two engage in a friendly discussion of a mutually interesting topic. However, the moment that the nature of the agent's business is divulged, Mr. Prospect goes on the defensive. Why? Because he fears that the agent may take too much of his time and may perhaps talk him into buying more insurance, which means more premiums to pay; or because he just does not want to listen to any proposition involving insurance. He does not know enough about the agent's offer to raise any objections to it; hence by use of the stalling objection he objects to giving the interview. Any one of the following might serve the purpose.

"Sorry, but I have to meet my wife in 20 minutes."

"Leave one of your circulars. I will look it over and call you in a few days."

"I just rang for my secretary. I must get my dictation off in the next half hour."

"I'm not interested now. See me in the fall. I'll be in the market for more life insurance at that time."

What should the agent do to avoid this early dismissal? First, she must make certain that it really is a stall rather than a sincere objection. She may quickly ascertain whether, for example, the first objection given above is sincere or just a stall by asking the prospect, "Oh, I'm sorry to have called at such an inconvenient time. May I see you 30 minutes this afternoon (or tomorrow morning)?" If the prospect is just stalling, he will immediately invent an excuse for not seeing the agent an another time. In that case the agent is fully justified in ignoring the stall and trying to secure the interview immediately. If the prospect readily agrees to meeting the agent at a definite time later, the assumption is warranted that he did have a date with his wife, and the agent should thank him for the appointment and leave. Should the prospect fail to keep the definite appointment, then perhaps he is employing that device to stall off the interview.

Many of the specific objections discussed later might be stalling or shielding objections; or they might be honest ones. It is not always easy to determine in which category an objection falls. If there is a doubt about this, treat it as if it were an honest objection, always reserving the right to change your opinion. Some salespeople, when they are sure or strongly suspect that an objection is a stall, just ignore it and go ahead.

Others, confronted with the old stall, "I'll have to talk it over with my partner," come back with "I have an idea that your partner would trust you to make the decision on a deal like this." Then they proceed to sell.

Sometimes the best way to handle a weak objection is to encourage the prospect to state it fully. The prospect may thus reveal how silly it sounds. Besides, he is often chiefly interested in getting it off his chest. In either case, the interview can proceed better after the objection has been voiced.

Caution should be exercised not to treat an honest refusal to act immediately as a stalling objection. Suppose that Mr. Prospect tries to conclude the interview by saying, "I like your deal. I will talk it over with my wife and call you in the next few days." It sounds like a stall; yet it may be a sincere. The sales rep will need to use tact in handling such objections, since an erroneous conclusion might antagonize the prospect sufficiently to prevent the sale. Ordinarily a question or two will test the sincerity of any objection that might be either a stall or a real objection.

Whatever the reason for concealing the real objection or obstacle to buying, you must be able to recognize false objections and stalls and then to uncover the real ones. Several techniques are used.

Asking questions. Questions encourage prospects to talk and, sooner or later, they are likely to reveal what is really holding them back.

Sometimes the sales rep may ask frankly: "Ms. Prospect, I feel that we aren't getting anywhere in our conference, and I'm afraid it is my fault. There must be something that I have failed to bring out clearly. If you would just tell me what it is, it might save us both quite a bit of time."

Some sales reps carry the practice still further. When the buyer says that he does not want the proposition, the sales rep queries, "Just what is your reason?" The prospect will offer an objection, in reply to which the sales rep asks, "Is that your only reason?" If the prospect says, "Yes," he has eliminated all others and virtually promised to buy if the obstacle to buying can be removed.

If the sales rep is reluctant to ask the nature of the prospect's objection, how can she discover it? Perhaps she can use slightly indirect questions, hinting at the probable objection and watching closely to see what effect the questions have upon the prospect. She might say, "The other day I was talking over my proposition with Mr. Jones, and we couldn't reach any conclusion until I had made clear to him our guarantee. Maybe you, too, would like to have me go a little deeper into that?" Then she could see if her remarks were well directed, for the prospect would be likely to give some sign that would enable her to know whether or not she had hit upon the right objection.

The salesperson may even more forcefully pry into certain touchy areas in which she has learned objections frequently lurk, thereby encouraging prospects to talk about what is bothering them.

One common technique is asking for the additional objections. After the prospect has voiced objections, the sales rep then says, "Now then, Mr. Jones, what else is really bothering you? Isn't there something else you don't like or want to know about my proposition?" The prospect is encouraged to reply with real objections, once he sees that he has not fooled the sales rep.

Validity of Objections

Many objections are perfectly valid; the prospect is speaking the truth. Some of these valid objections are answerable, while others are not. The unanswerable objections generally take one of two forms: (1) no money or (2) no need for the proposition. Unfortunately these are often used as excuses to cover some hidden objections; hence you must immediately determine whether they are valid or are merely excuses.

Of course, there are price limits beyond which a prospect is truly unable to go. It would be useless to try to sell a new Rolls-Royce or a million-dollar life insurance policy to someone making $100 a week. You would be unethical as well as foolish if you forced such a sale.

Valid objections to other phases of the proposition will be discussed in detail later. However, a word of caution is needed. There is a tendency among salespeople to treat all objections as invalid. This is unfortunate, for it frequently injects antagonism into the interview when the prospect realizes that his perfectly valid objection is being treated lightly by the salesperson.

An executive objects, "I've heard too many bad reports on the service your company gives. I am afraid that I just can't see giving my business to you."

Many salespeople would treat this as an untruth, but the fact may be that he has heard some bad reports on the firm. Notice that he says he has heard bad reports, not that the alleged poor service is a fact. The sales rep may be convinced that her firm gives excellent service so she immediately labels the objection as invalid. This is a mistake, for the prospect believes it to be valid, and it must be treated as such if it is to be successfully met.

Handling Price Objections

Price objections include price, terms, delivery, advertising allowances, services, and many other factors that directly bear on the out-of-pocket costs of the product.

When the prospect says, "Your price is too high," this may mean any one of several things. First, it may mean that in his opinion your product is not worth the price you are asking; it is not a good value. Or he may be saying, in effect, that "I haven't enough money to pay your price." This, of course, is a different matter, for it assumes that if the prospect did have sufficient money he would buy. Naturally, the way to handle this type of price objection is different from that required to answer the first. In the latter case, you would attempt to work out some plan of payment that would meet the prospect's financial requirements. In the former case, you would start building up the value of the product in the prospect's mind.

In other instances, the prospect may be saying, "I

think I can buy your product elsewhere for less money."
The prospect is sold on your product and would buy it
at your price if it weren't for these other opportunities
she has in mind. The techniques used to handle this
type of objection naturally vary still further from those
previously used.

Thus before you can hope to answer a price objection, you must first determine exactly what the prospect
is objecting to. It is necessary to determine whether the
price objection is one of value, lack of money, or competition.

Hidden quality or merits. The classic answer to
value objections has usually been to focus efforts on
increasing the merits of the product in the eyes of the
prospect. Many times the reasons for an item's higher
price are not obvious but must be specifically pointed
out. After all, if a product carries a legitimately higher
price, there must be some reason for it; therefore, prove
the reasons.

Sales representatives for a check writer, designed to
prevent checks from being raised, use this method
effectively: "I have a watch here. What would you
estimate it is worth? . . . you don't know because you
have not examined the works. That is true—you cannot
tell whether it is worth $10 or $100 merely by looking
at the outside. What is true of this watch is even more
true of our machine. Inside this machine are seven
segments, each with 10 individual dies of a hard com-
position, besides an oscillating and two stationary dies,
making 73 in all. Every character must be true to the
thousandth of an inch. This means the finest kind of
workmanship." From here the sales rep goes on to
explain the other hidden parts of the machine, stressing
quality all the way.

The salesperson for a manufacturer trying to sell to

a purchasing agent of another manufacturer may find it effective to say, "No doubt your own salespeople have to meet the same objection every day and they answer it in the same way I'm going to answer you. You believe that your product is good - that it is worth what you ask for it. You could probably cheapen it in places, but you don't want to sacrifice quality to do it. We are in exactly the same boat and I know you understand."

John Ruskin wrote nearly 100 years ago, "There is hardly anything in the world that some man cannot make a little worse and sell a little cheaper, and the people who consider the price only are this man's lawful prey."

Sometimes the idea that the product is truly of high quality can be established if you focus the prospect's attention on one key part or component and prove its quality beyond doubt, thus suggesting that the rest of the product is similarly constructed.

But, you protest, suppose the product is truly over-priced. It is not a good value. Then why are you representing it? Remember, we began this study by strongly maintaining that you must believe in what you are selling and for whom it is being sold. If you feel that your products are not good values, you'd better look for another job.

Savings or profits. Many times, particularly in selling to industrial concerns or middlemen, the qualities or merits of the product may be completely beside the point. The important factor business executives look for is the product's ability to save them money or make them a profit. Suppose a certain product cost only $100 to make and were of obviously cheap construction; however, it would save the prospect $6000 during the first year. Would the buyer refuse to pay $100 for it? In pricing theory, costs do not determine prices; the market does. Costs determine profits and therefore, who stays in business. You should not think that the price of your product must be justified on a cost basis, because often it will not be possible to do this. After all, it is often impossible to ascertain the costs of a certain product. Do forequarters of beef cost more than hindquarters? No, but they have to be priced differently in order to clear the market in equal amounts.

The best justification for a high price is that the product will save or make the buyer more than its price. If you can prove that fact, the prospect will buy.

Most industrial sales are built around the profit or savings that will accrue to the buyer. Once this has been convincingly demonstrated, price is seldom a barrier. IBM's electric typewriters are the highest priced line in the industry, but they are the leading seller. The Hughes Tool Company was able to obtain a handsome price for its rotary diamond drilling bit because it saved the oil well drilling contractor considerable money as compared with the old cable drilling method.

The best method for overcoming a price objection is to show that the product would not cost the buyer a cent; it would actually make money. If such is the case, you can reply to the objection, "I can't afford to buy it," with "You can't afford not to buy it."

Break down price into smaller units. Sometimes the high unit price of an item may scare the prospect into making a price objection without really giving thought to exactly how much is being asked for it.

Big price tags can be frightening regardless of the values they represent. Real estate salespeople continually encounter a great reluctance to make an offer by people to whom the high prices are frightening. Such amounts are beyond their comprehension even though the price may be quite reasonable for the property involved.

An adding machine salesperson says, "I have already shown you how you can save money by the purchase of one of our machines, but I see that I have not made myself clear in comparing the cost of this machine and the saving that it will give you. You have already told me that your loss through incorrect additions, etc. totals up to several cents per day. All right. Let's assume that you will wish to renew the machine every five years, by turning in the old machine on a new one and paying the balance in cash. The price of the machine is $350, and at the end of five years it can be turned in for about $100. That leaves you a cost of $250 over a period of five years, or $50 for one year. Dividing that by 300, the number of working days in a year, we have a cost of 16 ⅔ cents per day. Your present system is certainly costing you more than that, isn't it?"

The basic idea behind this breakdown technique is to quote the price on some other basis than the product itself. The price can be related to some short unit of time or to some unit of productivity. A paper sales rep made a sale of quality letterheads to a purchasing agent by saying, "Isn't it worth one-tenth of a cent to you to know that your firm is being represented on the best letterhead paper available? That's all it will cost to give you the best instead of what you are now buying."

Of course, one way to meet the price objection is to offer easy terms of payment, reducing the statement of the price to fractions of the original amounts.

Comparison. Often the prospect unfavorably reacts to price only as the result of not having carefully compared it with other products selling for similar prices. A father objected strenuously to the seemingly high price of a bicycle for his son until the sales rep asked, "How much did you pay for those golf clubs I see in your car? . . . Which do think it takes more time and effort to make, golf clubs or bicycles?" Since the man had just laid out $300 for his clubs, he had no alternative but to buy the bicycle.

When the price difficulty seems to be based on a comparison between your product and a competing one, it may be good strategy to get the exact difference between the two and then show clearly just what your product offers for the extra amount asked. In this way, by stressing exclusive advantages, the difference in price may be made to appear small.

A potential buyer of filing cabinets complained that he could buy another brand for $10 less than was being asked for a particularly well-known brand. The sales rep replied, "Let's see, you say that $10 is the difference between my brand and the one you have in mind. Let me show you what you are getting for your $10. First, our cabinets are 2 inches deeper, giving you about 8 percent more filing space. On a $50 investment that alone is worth $4. Next, if you will inspect the ball-bearing roller on which our drawers are mounted, you will find them much superior to the friction roller used in the other brand. Next, look at the way the movable support in each drawer is operated. Ours work much easier. Feel the way our drawers lock shut. It is obvious that this is quality hardware. So, you see, you are getting a lot of quality and superior performance for your $10."

Questioning. Questions can be effective in handling certain price objections. Many times a person believes a price to be high only because of ignorance or lack of thought about it. The right questions can encourage such prospects to realize that the price is in line, after all. The sales rep may ask such questions as, "Why do you think the price is out of line?" or "What price do you have in mind?" or "I wonder what you have in mind when you say our price is too high. High compared to what?"

Handling Procrastination

The motto of many people is never to do anything today that can be put off until tomorrow. Prospects frequently want to delay making a decision if they can. It would seem that making a decision to buy is a painful experience.

Admittedly, some procrastinations are legitimate. The prospect has to consult with some higher executive or has to wait for some event to happen, but most of them are just excuses.

Many procrastinations are offered as camouflage for other objections. Frequently, when the prospect says, "I think I'll look around some more" or "I'll have to think about it," what she is really saying is, "I am not at all persuaded that this is the deal for me." She remains unpersuaded; thus you must go back and discover her real objections.

The person who is unable to cope with procrastination will never be highly successful, for too many sales will be lost to more aggressive competitors.

There are several ways of handling procrastination.

Put a hook in the close. Many firms selling to middlemen always have a special deal for the rep to offer that is "good only on this call." There is ample cost justification for such inducements, for it costs money to have a sales rep make two or three calls to get an order that should have been gotten on the first call.

A machine tool sales rep would, when truthfully possible, put the following hook into his close. "There's a firm down in Wheeling that's been looking for a milling machine just like yours. I can unload it for you for a good trade-in if we can get going on this deal. Let me call right now and put together a deal for you."

What do you gain by waiting? Many times the prospect will see the light by simply comparing what is gained by waiting with what is lost. Usually he gains little or nothing, while the use of the product is lost for a period of time, not to speak of possible risks of price increases, and soon. Ask the prospect to write down exactly what is gained by waiting, while you write down what is lost.

Standing-room-only close. Supplies may be short, prices may be increased, models may change, or delivery dates may be altered. There are many reasons why you cannot always promise that your offer will be the same at a later date. Experience indicates that if the prospects don't act now, supplies will be unavailable by the time their decision is made, but many prospects do not believe it. Few things make a prospect want to buy quicker than the thought that he might not be able to buy later.

Sometimes impending events such as price increases, strikes, upturns in business activity, and model changes will create a situation on which you can capitalize to forestall the procrastinator. You can calmly mention these events during the presentation, thereby priming the prospect to buy promptly when he is convinced that the proposition is what is wanted.

In these inflationary times the ever-present threat of a price increase tacitly acts as an impeding event urging immediate action. Moreover, never underestimate the power of delivery dates to force buying actions from laggard purchasing agents. Few thoughts put such terror in the minds of purchasing agents as that of not having items in the plant when they are needed. Anything that threatens delivery can be used as an impending event to close a sale.

Now Close the Sale

A good salesperson is always a good closer, and a poor closer is always a poor salesperson. Everything that has gone before—prospecting, preapproach, approach, presentation, handling objections—all the preparation and effort have been focused on this objective. The sales rep who cannot close is like the runner who trains faithfully all season, leads the field in the big race until 10 yards from the tape, and then falls down.

The person who is uncertain of her closing abilities is handicapped throughout the presentation, for she cannot help being worried about the impending obstacle with which she has so much difficulty. Some people actually develop a fear of closing that eventually drives them out of selling. This usually comes about through a combination of ignorance of closing techniques and outright bashfulness about asking for the order. Many sales are made simply because the person had the fortitude to ask for the order.

Fear of Failure

Most of us are so psychologically programmed toward success that the mere thought of failure frightens us into a semiparalytic state in which we are afraid to ask for the order or final decision for fear of being refused. We seem to think that so long as we don't ask for the order we have avoided failure even though no sale transpires. We just do not like to hear such awful words as, "No!" "Not interested!" These terms bruise our egos, and that hurts us. Suppose the prospect does say "No." Really, that doesn't hurt you one bit. You can even learn to ignore it. If you cannot learn to take "no" for an answer and bounce right back without allowing it to affect your confidence, then you had better look somewhere else for a job.

Ineptness

Some salespeople just get so bogged down meeting objections that the thought of trying to close never enters their minds. They are fighting for their lives; they are confused; they have lost control of the sale. The close must be so natural to you that you swing into it automatically.

Cultural Taboos

Many people are raised in the tradition that it is improper to ask another person for money or to do something for you. Closing means asking for the order; thus it can run afoul of cultural taboos in some circles.

Closing Signals

If the prospect asks "How soon could you ship it?" this is a sign of real interest. It signals that it is time to close without going into more detail, even though you may not be finished with your presentation.

It has been said that, when prospects ask for the price, they are keenly interested; and that when they inquire about terms, they are practically ready to buy.

The Assumptive Close

The assumptive close is basic to every sale and should underlie all actions throughout the presentation, as well as at the time of closing. "The prospect is going to buy. There is no doubt about it!" These thoughts should be reflected in the sales rep's attitude and demeanor. Not that you should seem cocky or overconfident, but there should be no trace of doubt in your speech or actions that would indicate that there is a reason for not buying.

This is nothing more than the principle of positive suggestion applied to the closing of the sale. The sales rep assumes by word and act that the prospect has made up his mind to buy.

Any fact that must be determined to make the deal

can be used as the basis of an assumptive close. Many times action without words serves the same purpose, such as clearing a space on the desk to fill out the order blank, getting the pen ready, or merely pulling a chair up closer to the desk.

In the "physical action close" the sales rep by some physical action communicates to the prospect that she believes the proposition is acceptable to the prospect and all that remains is to complete the details. The essence of this tactic is action; get into action to indicate to the buyer that the matter is seemingly settled. The buyer has to make a special effort to stop the process, many buyers will fail to overcome their natural inertia, and so the sale is consummated. Just start writing the order.

Closing on a Minor Point
It is easier to make a minor decision than a major one, so make it easier for the prospect by avoiding the major decisions, "Yes, I will buy," and substituting a minor decision.

The industrial equipment representative might ask, "Are you interested in our lease plan or are you thinking of outright ownership?" thereby focusing the buyer's attention on this relatively minor point rather than the major issue of the acquisition itself.

Usually there are many minor issues to be decided by the prospect in a purchase; delivery dates, payment plans, optional features, and quantities required. Any of these factors can be used as a basis for closing.

Standing-Room-Only Close
Frequently the hesitating sale may be closed by what salespeople call "hanging out the SRO sign," the initials signifying, "Standing Room Only." People want

what others want. It is contrary to human nature to let an opportunity slip.

More than any of the other closing methods, the SRO plan attempts to scare the prospect because of a loss to be suffered if action is not taken immediately.

Industrial sales reps make frequent use of this technique with complete honesty. And by so doing, they are furnishing information that the prospect needs to make an intelligent decision. There may be some impending event, such as a strike, either in the seller's plant or in that of a supplier or a transport agent; or inventories may be running short in that particular model; or the special deal will be discontinued after this week; or some other event may occur that will prevent the prospect from exercising free choice at a later time.

Offering Special Inducement to Buy Now

This technique was referred to earlier as putting a hook in your close. It is used widely to encourage prospects to buy now.

It is important not to use this technique as a trick. The same inducement should not be used twice on the same prospect, or the prospect will quickly see that he could have had the premium whether or not he had bought at that time. But, judiciously employed, this is a highly effective way to prod some prospects into prompt action.

The Minnesota Mining and Manufacturing salespeople usually have a special inducement to offer dealers if they will buy some package deal today; on one trip they were giving the dealer a billfold.

Asking for the Order

In discussing methods for closing the sale, we are likely to overlook the perfectly obvious point—ask the prospect to buy. Professional buyers declare that it is amazing how many salespeople seem unable to bring themselves to ask for the order. Perhaps they are afraid of being turned down; maybe they forget to do it.

When the sale has been conducted on a rather matter-of-fact basis, it is natural for the salesperson to say, "Can I get your purchase order number right now for my order form?"

Under the right conditions, a flat statement declaring that the prospect ought to buy may be effective, such as "That seems to cover everything. You can OK the order right there."

Naturally the salesperson must know the prospect, but it is surprising the results one can get by forceful requests for the order.

Closing on an Objection or the Trap Close

The trap close, sometimes known as closing on an objection, can be effectively used when the prospect voices only one significant objection and the sales rep knows that it can be answered to the prospect's complete satisfaction.

Trap closes are used frequently in handling price objections. It is a serious error to give way on price without getting the prospect committed to buy if the price is met, as the prospect may continue to press for even larger concessions if his first demand is met. So the sales rep says, "Let's write up the proposition with the price you mentioned and just see what the office will do with it. You've nothing to lose that way, and who knows, maybe we can really get you a deal today. Never know how the boss feels; he might accept this contract." Once the prospect has signed for the lower price, if the seller agrees to it, the deal is binding.

The Follow-Up

The purpose of the follow-up is to make certain that the buyer is as completely satisfied with a purchase as it is possible to be. This applies to all buyers, whether they are expected to become regular customers or whether they will never buy again from you personally.

There are many factors that may govern the scope, intensity, and duration of the follow-up.

The importance of the sale is perhaps the chief factor. Obviously, someone who has just sold a magazine subscription cannot afford to call back several times to educate the customer in how to get the most pleasure from that magazine. But when the sale is a big one, it may be vitally important that the buyer be educated to extract the utmost in satisfaction from the purchase. The price paid probably includes a margin for this service, and the buyer is entitled to it.

A second factor is the likelihood of repeat business. If a long-time relationship is hoped for, with frequent and profitable orders, a follow-up that will develop the desired permanent relationship should be given.

A third factor may be termed "educational." Whatever the item is that is sold, if it need special knowledge and definite performance techniques on the part of operators or sales clerks, it is the salesperson's job to follow up that sale until sure that the product is being handled right. Ignorant or slipshod personnel may ruin the success of the installation and create a very unhappy customer who will go out of his way to knock the product and kill chances of making other sales.

With the foregoing thoughts in mind, one must strike a balance between active selling effort and follow-up activities. The test of whether you should devote a given hour to selling or to follow-up is simply—which way of spending that hour will result in more sales in the long run, because the basic purpose of any follow-up is to increase sales. A sales rep is not being altruistic; that time is not being given away. Rather, it is being invested in the manner that will bring great sales.

Examples of what you may be getting in return for an investment of your time:

1. You can gain the goodwill of the buyer by checking up to make sure that the order will be filled and delivered properly. This is especially necessary when the sale is the first one made to that buyer.

2. Retailers cannot accurately forecast demand, especially for a new product or line. The salesperson can, when following up the sale, help the dealer adjust the order, adding some here and perhaps taking back a little somewhere; and more often than not it is possible to add to the original order. In industrial selling, conditions can change quickly as new orders come in or new contracts are signed, so the salesperson who is on the job can often add to the original order when following up the sale.

3. A buyer who does not know how to operate or use the new purchase will be unhappy and may even return it. It takes a wise person to admit he does not understand something. The wise sales rep will understand this and take care to test covertly the buyer's comprehension of the equipment, such as making sure he can operate it by himself.

4. Present customers are a good source of leads for new business. The sales rep who follows up promptly on a sale can often catch the customer at the time when she can recall easily the names

of several friends with whom she has been discussing her recent purchase.

5. A later check on satisfaction is made some time after the first type of follow-up, and it has for its purpose the creation of goodwill and the procurement of new prospect's names.

6. One important gain from a good follow-up is the holding of customers in line or keeping from shifting to another source of supply.

7. The purpose of the follow-up is to lead into the next sale to the same buyer. This next sale may come at once or years later, but the smart sales rep is starting it the minute he follows up on any sale.

8. A satisfied customer is a firm's best advertisement; and every top-flight sales rep knows that he can trace much new business to the kind words uttered by some customer who appreciated the efforts of the sales rep to make certain that this customer was completely satisfied in his dealings with both the sales rep and his firm.